Preaching With All Our Souls

Preaching With All Our Souls

A *Study in Hermeneutics and Psychological Type*

Leslie Francis

and

Andrew Village

continuum

Continuum
The Tower Building   80 Maiden Lane
11 York Road   Suite 704
London   New York
SE1 7NX   NY 10038

www.continuumbooks.com

First published 2008

British Library Cataloguing-in-Publication Data
A catalogue record for this book is available from the British Library.

ISBN 9-780-8264-9326-2

Designed and typeset by Kenneth Burnley, Wirral, Cheshire.
Printed and bound by MPG Books Ltd, Bodmin, Cornwall.

Contents

Preface

This is a book about the theory of preaching written by two Anglican priests who are used to preaching Sunday by Sunday. For us the real test of the theory has been its practical relevance to our ministry. This is a theory about what we are doing when we preach, why we are doing it, and how we do it. A number of factors and a number of individuals have helped to shape what we do and how we have come to give an account of what we do in this book. Above all, our gratitude goes to those congregations who have nurtured our vocation and challenged our assumptions.

Leslie Francis wishes to record his gratitude especially to Tony Crockett who first challenged him to think through the application of psychological type theory for clergy development, to Peter Atkins who challenged him to think more deeply about the relationship between psychological type theory and contemporary debates in hermeneutical theory, and to Susan Jones, John Payne and Mandy Williams-Potter who worked with him on structuring and delivering a number of practical workshops in these areas. Eventually, however, it was conversations with Andrew Village which helped the different strands of theory and experience to fall into place and to make good coherent sense.

Andrew Village wishes to record his gratitude especially to the congregations in which he has worshipped and served as deacon and priest, and which allowed him to pursue both parish ministry and academic study. Out of this grew an interest in the Bible and its interpretation, and from this an interest in hermeneutics and preaching. This interest was fostered in no small part by Leslie Francis, who generously made room in this project for a second author.

Both authors wish to record their gratitude to those who have helped to shape the present manuscript – Susan Thomas, Diane Drayson and

Mandy Robbins – and to Robin Baird-Smith for commissioning the book and for waiting so patiently for its completion.

Leslie J. Francis
University of Warwick

Andrew Village
York St John University

Introduction

This is a book designed for preachers and is about preaching. It is a practical book designed to equip those individuals who have responded to (or who are thinking about responding to) the call to be preachers to become better preachers. It is a practical book because it is fully grounded in a theory about the nature of preaching.

Both authors are seasoned preachers and privileged preachers. We are seasoned preachers because our vocation is to ministry among the congregations we are called to serve. Sunday by Sunday we read the text of scripture, reflect on the text and preach on the basis of our reflection. We are privileged preachers because our day-job in the academy invites us to reflect on the task of ministry, to research the fields of hermeneutics, homiletics, catechetics and Christian formalities. We earn our living as practical and empirical theologians.

In this book we want to invite fellow preachers (and trainee preachers) to come on a journey of discovery with us. The journey takes us into two fields of established knowledge. In the first part of the journey we explore the field of hermeneutics in general and biblical hermeneutics in particular. Hermeneutics is concerned with the quest for meaning, and with the discovery of how the message is shaped and interpreted. Many have made that journey before us, but our perspective on the journey is new. Our perspective forces us to recognize the crucial role that psychology can play in this quest for meaning.

In the second part of the journey we explore the field of personality psychology in general and psychological type in particular. Personality psychology is concerned with understanding individual differences, and with the discovery of how personality may shape our perceptions and evaluations of the message. Many have made the journey before us, but once again our perspective on the journey is now. Our perspective forces us to recognize how individual differences of this nature are part of God's plan for engaging with God's revelation.

The purpose of the journey is simple. If preachers really take seriously current knowledge about hermeneutics, if preachers really attend to what is known about psychological type, and if preachers apply this knowledge to practice, their approach to preaching will be radically transformed.

In this book we draw on hermeneutical theory and on psychological type theory to introduce what we have come to describe as 'the SIFT method of biblical hermeneutics and liturgical preaching'. If we are correct in our integration of these two fields, what we are proposing is a highly distinctive and creatively radical approach to preaching. This approach provides preachers with a framework and structure in which they can have confidence. This approach releases the gospel message to be proclaimed and to be heard in a full and rounded manner.

The SIFT method of biblical hermeneutics and liturgical preaching draws on the model of the human psyche proposed by psychologist Carl Jung. Jung maintains that the human psyche (which can be translated 'wind' or 'soul') embraces four key psychological functions defined as Sensing, Intuition, Feeling and Thinking. In the course of normal human development each individual tends to develop one of these functions more strongly then the other three. This becomes known as that individual's dominant function. Each of these four functions dialogues with the text of scripture (and with the revelation of scripture) in its own distinctive way. We take the gospel command to 'love the Lord your God with all your mind, with all your soul' as an invitation to ensure that we both read and proclaim the text of scripture giving equal attention to all four psychological functions. It is this distinctive emphasis of the SIFT method of biblical hermeneutics and liturgical preaching that leads to our title: *Preaching With All Our Souls*. On our account, it is simply not sufficient for preachers to encounter the text of scripture through their own preferred dominant function. They need to learn to open up their minds, to open up their souls, in order to read the text and to proclaim the message in light of the insights of the four functions.

After setting the foundations in theory, this book concludes by displaying the SIFT method in practice. And on the way, preachers are given the practical opportunity to make an assessment of their own psychological type and to reflect on the implications of that information for the ways in which they read and proclaim scripture.

Part 1

Preaching and Hermeneutics

Chapter 1

Preaching and Meaning

Introduction

In Britain, if you tune to BBC Radio Four at 5.55 p.m. on Long Wave you may hear something like this:

> Forties Cromarty Forth Tyne southerly veering north westerly 4 or 5 increasing 6 or 7 for a time rain for a time good becoming moderate.

If you did not know what this was, you might have some difficulty in interpreting what you were hearing. It might make more sense if you knew it was the Shipping Forecast, but even then you would need to work hard to decipher what is a quite complex code. First you would need to recognize that 'Forties Cromarty Forth Tyne' refers to different parts of the inshore waters around Britain, and you would need to know where these are. Then you would need to realize that 'southerly veering north westerly 4 or 5 increasing 6 or 7' refers to the wind. You would need considerable background knowledge to know what 'veering' means (as opposed to 'backing') and that the numbers refer to the Beaufort scale of wind speed. You might also wonder why 'rain for a time' was 'good', unless you knew that the adjective was referring to visibility, not rain.

The Shipping Forecast is a message, and the Greek god Hermes was said (among other things) to be the messenger who transmitted the thoughts and intentions of the gods to mortals. The idea of Hermes as messenger led to the term 'hermeneutics', which describes the study of 'messages' in their broadest sense. It is the study of communication and how we make sense of what we hear or read. As such, hermeneutics is integral to preaching and important for preachers, so this chapter introduces some of the key ideas and recent developments in hermeneutics.

Hermeneutics for preachers

The Shipping Forecast is an example of a very dense message that is coded to convey the maximum amount of information with the minimum amount of words. It must be utterly clear and unambiguous to those for whom it is intended, for lives may depend on it. It succeeds insofar as the producers (the Meteorological Office) and the intended recipients (sailors) both understand the code and can translate weather conditions into the code and vice versa. If you listen to the whole forecast and know where the shipping areas are and what the rest means, you should be able to get a clear picture of the weather of the inshore waters of the British Isles on a particular day. This is what the Shipping Forecast means.

Or is it? In 2002 it was decided that one of the shipping areas should change its name from Finisterre to Fitzroy. This simple change should have caused little disruption, provided that both Meteorological Office and sailors knew the part of the sea to which the new name referred. It was odd, then, that the change caused outrage among some listeners to Radio Four who had never set foot in a fishing boat and who had no idea where Finisterre was. People demanded that the change be stopped and the row spilled onto the news programmes for a day or so (at least on Radio Four). The BBC website had an obituary that began 'R.I.P. Finisterre shipping forecast sea area, a familiar friend taken away from us after a lifetime of service.' This was clearly not aimed at sailors, who probably could not have cared less about the change; it was aimed at people who had embraced the Shipping Forecast in a completely different context and for completely different reasons.

In Britain, the Shipping Forecast has become more than a coded message about the weather. Broadcast for years to people for whom it was not originally intended, its familiar words, rhythm and cadences sank into hearts and minds. People who had no idea of the code and no interest in ships or weather nonetheless came to regard it as having meaning for them. It has been satirized, has featured in song lyrics and has inspired art exhibitions. This 'leakage of meaning' is a good illustration of the fact that meaning is complex and not easily controlled. If this is true of an apparently simple message like the Shipping Forecast, how much more complex will be the message(s) of religion?

Preachers are people with a message, so hermeneutics intersects with preaching in several different ways. Hermeneutics in this context is about the messages that preachers perceive, shape and transmit, and the way those messages are understood by audiences. Hermeneutics has something to say about the creation of messages. The preacher's 'message' may be broadly conceived and broadly sourced, emerging from a complex interaction of people, traditions and a sacred text. It may be a general message such as 'the gospel' or the specific message of a particular sermon.

Hermeneutics also has something to say about how messages are encoded and transmitted. This aspect is especially important for preachers because they are people who have to deliver their message in a particular code (the sermon) and in a particular context (the preaching of that sermon). The way in which a message is encoded and transmitted can become part of the message itself, and often the message is so closely entwined with the medium that it is impossible to convey it in any other way. Saying a psalm is very different from chanting it. Preaching is a more varied medium in these days of video projectors and surround-sound systems, but the vast majority of preaching uses the traditional format of a preacher talking to a congregation. This way of encoding and delivering messages carries with it expectations that are often closely tied to the person who is preaching. In many ways, the preacher *is* the medium, and it is naïve to assume that the two can be easily separated. Hermeneutics is partly about the way in which the message is shaped by, and dependent upon, the messenger.

Hermeneutics also has something to say about the reception of messages. What is conveyed may be the message that was intended by the preacher, but as we have seen from the example of the Shipping Forecast, intentions do not always control final outcomes. Most preachers know only too well the experience of having a carefully explained and nuanced message fed back to them at the church door in a way that makes it totally unrecognizable, or even worse, the exact opposite of what was intended. Recent hermeneutical studies have wrestled with the extent to which recipients create their own meaning as opposed to decoding it from the message.

So hermeneutics is likely to have something to say to preachers. The last 50 years have seen profound developments in the field of hermeneutics and these have spilled over into academic religious circles, changing completely the way in which the Bible is interpreted. The story of these developments is now widely understood and has been told and retold in many different ways. It is a story in which the dominance of historical method gave way to a plethora of reading styles derived from increasingly sophisticated (some might say arcane) approaches that were much more self-consciously aware of the complexities of meaning. Just as the Shipping Forecast has come to operate at all sorts of levels and in ways never originally intended, so the Bible has generated meanings that would have been incomprehensible to scholars of just a few generations ago, let alone to those who wrote it. These changes have spilled out from the academic world into some parts of the Church where they have begun to affect the outlook and work of preachers. Other parts of the Church have remained more or less unmoved by the currents of change, and preaching continues in ways that proponents argue are faithful to God and to the sacred text, and which others argue are increasingly becoming marginalized in Western societies.

It is our contention that preachers need to be aware of the trends in academic hermeneutics and ideally to learn something from them. At times the debates within the field seem to be nothing more than the in-house musing of academics who have lost touch with real religious life. Yet they concern important issues and are linked to currents of change that affect both established members of congregations and those who might join them. Preachers who ignore the ways in which people understand what they hear or read are likely to find themselves preaching only to those who can be sustained by a particular and narrow genre of communication. This is sometimes referred to as 'preaching to the converted': increasingly it is precisely *not* preaching to people who have been converted, it is preaching to people who have always been part of a particular Church tradition. Potential converts simply do not understand what preachers are saying.

Biblical hermeneutics

Those who study hermeneutics sometimes separate 'general' hermeneutics, the study of meaning across a range of discourses, from 'special' hermeneutics, which are particular to a given area of discourse. Biblical studies were for a long time considered to be an area of 'special hermeneutics', requiring unique and particular methods to interpret the sacred text. In the eyes of many biblical exegetes, the notion that the Bible is in some sense divine revelation sets it apart from other texts and demands that it be treated differently. However, the underlying trend in biblical studies has been for the assumptions and methods of general hermeneutics to invade the territory of biblical interpretation. These days, interpretation of the Bible is as likely to draw on methods that derive from philosophy or literary studies as from traditional exegesis. For some, this represents a sell-out to secularism, while for others it enables the Bible to speak across religious boundaries. Whatever the merits of this change, the developments in general hermeneutics have had a profound impact on biblical hermeneutics. Before looking at some general lessons that can be gleaned from current biblical hermeneutics, it is worth outlining briefly the state of the art. Those who want a more thorough overview of the philosophical currents that have shaped biblical interpretation are referred to the work of Anthony Thiselton (1980, 1992), while Bray (1996) offers a useful historical review.

The trend in biblical studies since the 1970s has been for historical-critical approaches to be joined by an increasing array of literary-critical or ideological approaches that stress the importance of readers in creating meaning. Historical approaches have by no means died out, but now share the field with a host of new techniques that all vie for attention in the same crowded patch of academia. The various approaches are now so well documented and described that only a brief summary and illustration is needed here. Useful description and discussion of some of these methods can be found in Adam (1995), Anderson and Moore (1992), Barton (1998), Coggins and Houlden (1990), Gillingham (1998), Haynes and McKenzie (1999), Hayes (1999), McCartney and Clayton (1994), Shillington (2002) and Tate (1997) among others.

To illustrate some different methods, we will use a passage from the Gospel of Mark that is not wholly unconnected to the analogy of the Shipping Forecast. Mark 4.35–41 recounts a story of Jesus and his disciples crossing the Sea of Galilee. It has been a long day of teaching by the shore, and Jesus suggests they leave the crowds behind to cross to the other side of the lake. A sudden windstorm threatens to sink the boat, yet Jesus sleeps soundly on a cushion in the stern. It is only when he is woken that he rebukes the wind and commands the sea to be still, so that a flat calm prevails. 'Why are you afraid? Have you no faith?', asks Jesus. His companions, filled with awe, have a question of their own: 'Who then is this, that even the wind and the sea obey him?'

On that day, when evening had come, he said to them, 'Let us go across to the other side.' And leaving the crowd behind, they took him with them in the boat, just as he was. Other boats were with him. A great windstorm arose, and the waves beat into the boat, so that the boat was already being swamped. But he was in the stern, asleep on the cushion; and they woke him up and said to him, 'Teacher, do you not care that we are perishing?' He woke up and rebuked the wind, and said to the sea, 'Peace! Be still!' Then the wind ceased, and there was a dead calm. He said to them, 'Why are you afraid? Have you still no faith?' And they were filled with great awe and said to one another, 'Who then is this, that even the wind and the sea obey him?' (Mark 4.35–41, NRSV)

Historical-critical approaches

Historical-critical studies seek the world 'behind' the text, mining it for clues that reveal its origin, construction and purpose. In our Shipping Forecast analogy, the aim would be to crack the code and work back to understand the offshore weather on a given day. Trying to understand what the author intended is of crucial importance. Biblical authors are assumed to have had a particular viewpoint on the cultural and religious landscape of the time, and this viewpoint shaped what they wrote and why they wrote it. Understanding the world of the author is therefore the key to understanding the meaning of the text.

Early historical studies such as source, form or redaction criticism used the text as the primary source of information, assuming that current versions hide within them the complex layers of their history. Recent historical methods such as social-scientific criticism rely more heavily on evidence beyond the text itself. Such evidence comes from disciplines such as archaeology, anthropology and sociology, which are helping to produce increasingly sophisticated understandings of ancient cultures.

Historical analysis of Mark 4.35–41 would look for the origin of the story: was this something based on an event in the life of Jesus, or was it a story largely created and shaped by the early Christian community? If the latter, was it a story formed from historical antecedents, or was it created for a particular purpose, such as encouraging believers in diffi-cult times? Some interpreters have emphasized the links of this story to Old Testament stories such as Jonah (who was thrown into the sea to calm the storm), or to the general notion of God ruling the sea or the chaos monster associated with the sea (see Geyer, 2002; Taylor, 1966). Others have seen wider roots for this imagery by suggesting there was a general notion of sleeping or resting as characteristics associated with divinity in the Ancient Near East (Batto, 1987). A more direct historical context might have been the persecution of the early Church, suggesting that the author intended the story to be interpreted symbolically. Cranfield (1959), for example, points out that the ship was a very early symbol of the Church in Christian art, and there would have been an obvious parallel between the situation of the disciples on the lake and the Church in the midst of persecution. What links these different approaches is that they are trying to understand how first- or second-century readers would have understood this story.

Historical analyses tend to be characterized by a positive attitude to the collection and objective assessment of empirical data. Whether the data are particular features of the text or evidence from extra-textual sources, historical approaches assume that the world of the author is both accessible and understandable. As such, historical criticism is rightly seen as a child of the sort of Enlightenment rationalism that typified modernity.

Literary-critical approaches

Historical methods of biblical interpretation were joined in the early 1970s by literary methods, which took their lead from the New Criticism and Structuralism developed by secular literary scholars in the early to mid-twentieth century. The aim of literary analysis is to understand how the words, structures and images in the text combine to shape meaning. A literary analysis of the Shipping Forecast might seek to explain the codes and how they allow forecasters to influence the activities of sailors. Alternatively they might recognize and accept that this original purpose has been subverted and instead analyse the forecast as poetry, paying attention to the unintended rhythms and ambiguities that are apparent once the text is removed from its original context.

This sort of literary approach remains rooted in the philosophical outlook of modernity, with the assumption that literary structures are objective entities that point to meanings that are transferred from author to readers. Literary critics focus on the conventions of genre that might be understood by authors and readers, and on the structures of narrative, poetry and rhetoric. They refer to 'implied' authors and 'implied' readers to denote the set of shared competencies and conventions that would allow a particular text to be understood. These are not 'real' authors or 'real' readers, but imaginary figures whose writing or reading strategies are implied by the literary analysis of the text.

Literary analysis of Mark 4.35–41 might pick up on the motifs used by the author to carry meaning and create atmosphere, and that might be recognized by the intended readers. Elizabeth Malbon (1992) points out that the narrator of Mark is careful to set his scenes, which have different connotations and various associations with Old Testament stories. The 'mountain' is where God meets the leaders of the people, and is where the Transfiguration takes place; the 'wilderness' is where God shows divine care in miraculously feeding the people, and is where the Feeding of the 5,000 occurs. The 'sea' is the place where God manifests divine power, and this is the context for the Stilling of the Storm.

In Mark's narrative a change of scene often coincides with a significant movement in the overall plot. The sea is the dominant scene in Mark 4, but, as the story of the storm ends, the scene moves on to the far shore. Coinciding with this change, the reader is left with a question: 'Who then is this, that even the wind and the sea obey him?' Literary critics have pointed out that the question of the identity of Jesus is a key thread that runs through Mark's Gospel (for example, see Matera, 1988), so this final question is crucial and demands an answer. None is given at the time, but the implied reader would share with the author knowledge of Psalm 107, which refers to Yahweh who calmed the storm. The implication is that Jesus has divine attributes, and a literary analysis of the Stilling of the Storm places it in the wider context of the unfolding identity of Jesus in the Markan narrative.

Literary critics may still have to delve into the history of the text, but, in contrast to historical scholars, would see history as a means rather than an end. For example, historical analysis may help to show if certain genres or literary conventions were widely used at the time a text was written, and were therefore likely to be deliberate ploys used by the author. Even where there is little historical evidence to show this was so, literary critics will not shy away from suggesting ways in which formal conventions create meaning, for the end goal is always to understand better the world 'in the text'.

Reader-centred approaches

Once meaning was thought to be independent of authors, it was not long before attention turned to readers. Implied readers were imaginary people who read texts with a particular competency and were, therefore, able to inhabit the world created by those texts. At first, rather little attention was given to seeing if real 'flesh and blood' readers would actually identify and respond to the literary devices that scholars claimed were in the text. Eventually, however, both literary critics and some cognitive psychologists began to ask just how texts affect readers, which has led to empirical studies of reading that have been growing steadily since the 1980s.

Another reason for the interest in 'real' readers has been the development of ideologically driven ways of interpreting the Bible. Feminist, liberation, black (now African-American) and post-colonial approaches all stress the importance of the social location of readers in shaping meaning (Segovia and Tolbert, 1995a, 1995b). Along with the growth of what is generally termed 'cultural studies' (Easthope, 1991; Guerin, Labor, Morgan, Reesman and Willingham, 2005; Segovia, 1995) these approaches emphasize that what a text means often depends on what sort of people are reading it and their particular social background.

With such diverse origins for 'reader-centred' approaches, it is not surprising that it is difficult to find a single method of interpretation to apply to a given text. Indeed, reader-centred approaches tend deliberately to avoid 'method'. Reading Mark 4.35–41 from this perspective might suggest obvious symbolic links between the storm-tossed disciples and difficult times in the lives of those reading the text today. This is not unlike suggestions made by historical critics about how this story may have operated for persecuted Christians in its original setting. The difference is that 'persecution' for some contemporary Western Christians might mean something very different from what is meant in the first century, and few contemporary readers are likely to understand the possible historical allusions to sleeping gods or the God who stills the raging waters. Nonetheless, modern readers are likely to see in this story a metaphor of their own storm-tossed lives, and take from it the message that calmness will prevail for those who have faith.

These literary and ideological reader-centred approaches have been joined by others that either directly draw on postmodern insights (Adam, 1995; Aichele, Burnett, Castelli, Fowler, Jobling, Moore, Phillips, Pippin, Schwartz and Wuellner, 1995), or are heavily influenced by the individuality of the reader (Kitzberger, 1999). In contrast to historical or literary approaches, reader-centred approaches to biblical studies are less interested in extracting objective meaning from the text and more interested in the meanings that readers create. The stress on pluralism, subjectivity and the enculturation of meaning leads to a very different understanding of the purpose and end-goal of biblical interpretation. It is less about extracting timeless truths from the text and more about the text being drawn into the world of the reader, the world 'in front of the text'.

Theological approaches

The previous approaches have shown how the concerns of general or secular hermeneutics have influenced the interpretation of the Bible in academic circles. Alongside these different approaches, and intersecting with them to a varying extent, has been the continuing claim of faith-based scholars that the Bible is different from other texts and must be treated differently. Theological interpretation starts from the assumption that the text reveals God and therefore carries particular or unique authority. Theological approaches therefore buck the trend by insisting that the Bible cannot be interpreted like any other text (see, for example, Adam, Fowl, Vanhoozer and Watson, 2006). By definition, theological approaches are the product of faith communities, but theological interpreters are found in secular universities as well as in theological colleges and churches. In churches, interpretation has always been driven largely by prior theological commitments to the nature of God and the nature of scripture. In academic circles, theological interpreters have sometimes had to fight to justify their place in state-funded universities (see, for example, the debate between Watson, 1994 and Davies, 1995). Against a backdrop of hermeneutical approaches that stress the way in which human motives and actions have shaped the production and interpretation of the Bible, theologians have continued to assert that this is not an entirely human enterprise.

Precisely how the Bible is understood in terms of revelation varies enormously between theologians, and the details need not concern us here. The main point to note is that preaching is an activity of faith communities, where the message is understood not simply as the words of the preacher, but also as the Word of God. Theological approaches to hermeneutics have shown something of a resurgence in recent years, and a growing number of scholars assert the right of faith-based interpretations of scripture to have a place in both academy and church.[1] Kevin Vanhoozer (1998) goes so far as to suggest that it is the Trinitarian nature of God that is the prerequisite for all communication and therefore the basis of both general and special hermeneutics. While few interpreters might go this far, it nonetheless shows the way in which faith-based interpreters take seriously the idea that God communicates to people. This communication is not confined to the biblical text, and some theological interpreters argue that it embraces the whole activity of the people of God (for example, Adam, Fowl, Vanhoozer and Watson, 2006). Given the origins of the word 'hermeneutics', from Hermes the messenger between the gods and humans, this seems entirely appropriate. Hermeneutics for preachers is about understanding the way in which God is revealed through many different sources.

Conclusion

If hermeneutics is the study of the way in which messages are created, transmitted and interpreted, then it must be an important concern for preachers. We have noted that hermeneutics in general has been dominated by a shift in emphasis from those methods that relied heavily on historical analysis to those that centre on the way in which readers create meaning. The same passage can be analysed in different ways, so that different sorts of messages can be gleaned from it. Preachers need to be aware of their own assumptions and experience when they come to create sermons. Some may use a biblical text as a window to the past, and try to help their listeners to understand that world. Others might analyse the way in which the writer has told a story, and try to allow the story to speak powerfully to a new generation of listeners. Yet others might be aware of the lives of their listeners, and try to make the text relevant to a specific context. Wise preachers may use a combination of these approaches within the same sermon or from one sermon to another.

All preachers are likely to have some sense that what they are doing is a theologically driven task of trying to understand and communicate divine revelation. It is the prior assumptions about the nature of hermeneutics that may govern the way in which preachers go about the task of preaching, and the particular methods they employ to create their messages. Before they communicate a message, preachers must create that message; before they speak they must listen; before they write they must read. The next chapter looks at how hermeneutical theory can help preachers to understand themselves as readers.

Chapter 2

Preachers as Readers

Introduction

The previous chapter provided a brief overview of developments in the methods used to interpret texts in general and the Bible in particular. These changes in method reflect broader, underlying changes in the perception of what it means to interpret texts and the world around us. In part, the changes reflect philosophical shifts in Western societies that have raised questions about the nature of meaning and the interpretation of reality. Interpretation, at a broad level, is a central task for those who preach, so the philosophical debate about hermeneutics is one that necessarily impinges on the craft of preaching. The reaction against the certainties of objective and absolute truth, which lies at the heart of postmodernity, has made hermeneutics a crucial part of a wider philosophical debate. Indeed, for postmodernists all truth is interpretation. Others disagree and maintain that humans have the capacity to identify and respond to objective reality. The philosophical roots of the current debate in hermeneutics are manifold and complex, and not within the scope of this book. However, a brief look at some of these roots is crucial to put what follows later in a broader context. This summary is drawn mainly from the work of Anthony Thiselton (1980, 1992), who has done more than anyone to place biblical interpretation in its philosophical and historical contexts.

Hermeneutical theory

Friedrich Schleiermacher (1768–1834) was an important figure in developing hermeneutical theory at a time when historical approaches to the Bible were rapidly gaining momentum. For Schleiermacher, interpretation was the process of getting into the minds of authors: standing in their shoes and thinking their thoughts after them. He recognized that this was partly about grammatical exegesis (understanding of the grammar of the language in which a text is written) and partly about philology (understanding the different possible meanings of words), so that a given text must be studied closely to determine the meaning of each particular phrase and clause. The paradox with an ancient text like the Bible is that the meaning of the whole depends on the meaning of the parts, but the parts themselves may only make sense in the wider context to which they belong. For example, in Mark's account of the Stilling of the Storm, when Jesus commands the storm to cease he uses the Greek word for 'muzzle' (*phimoo*). This verb broadly means to 'tie up', and is used to refer to muzzling oxen who are threshing corn (1 Corinthians 9.9 and 1 Timothy 5.18), but it is also used figuratively to refer to people who have been silenced (Matthew 22.34, Jesus silences the Sadducees). The figurative use of the word elsewhere helps to make sense of its use in Mark 4.39 (where Jesus commands the sea to 'be muzzled!' meaning 'be silenced!'), and its use in this case also helps to broaden the understanding of the different ways in which this particular word is used in a figurative sense. So discernment proceeds in a circle, the 'hermeneutical circle', of bringing wider knowledge to bear on individual texts, which in turn shape that wider knowledge.

Schleiermacher also had a more romantic side, and recognized that getting into the mind of the author was a skill that could not be wholly described by the rational analysis of textual information. There was also the art of 'divination', which defies precise description but which allowed for a certain intuition on the part of the interpreter. This is akin to getting to know a friend, and points to a more psychological analysis of the author rather than a rational, grammatical analysis of the text. This combination of objective and subjective analysis should, argued Schleiermacher, allow the interpreter to understand the text as well as, or even better than, the author. This is an important insight that reminds us that interpretation requires different psychological processes: some are rational, some are intuitive, some are based on detached analysis and some are based on a more personal engagement.

This optimism about being able to stand in the author's shoes, as it were, pervaded the generations of historical scholars who followed Schleiermacher. On the whole there was an assumption that the methods and objectives of historical enquiry were both legitimate and attainable. This consensus began to unravel during the twentieth century as a number of independent philosophical movements chipped away at both rational and romantic views of what it meant to understand ancient texts. A key figure was Hans Georg Gadamer, whose book *Truth and Method,* published in the early 1960s, crystallized the growing unease with the idea that the author's intent was the sole arbiter of meaning (Gadamer, 1960). Once an author's or artist's work is produced, he or she does not necessarily have the sole right to decide what it means.

Gadamer stressed the 'horizon' of interpreters, which defines the limits within which we are able to understand. He argued that going beyond those horizons is not possible and it is naïve to assume that we can really understand any text or aesthetic creation as it would have origin-ally been understood. Gadamer's work reminds us that we inhabit a different world from that which created the biblical text, but also shows that we can only comprehend a text through the lens of previous gener-ations. We cannot escape the effects of how texts have previously been interpreted by trying to leapfrog back to the original authorial intention. Nor should we, argued Gadamer, for what is the point of understanding something without reference to our own times and our own horizon? That is not interpretation because interpretation means understanding the object in relation to the culture and times of the interpreter.

Gadamer did not want to abandon the past, but rather sought to encourage interpretation that was aware of the different ways in which a text had been interpreted and was able to appreciate it in ways that were meaningful for the present generation. Gadamer's work is important in showing that interpreting texts is more than simply finding out what they meant to those who wrote them: it is about the way in which these objects are then 're-presented' in different generations in order for them to have a continuing meaning. Interpretation is always about re-reading into a particular context.

Gadamer's sophisticated and comprehensive analysis gave philosoph-ical ballast to those who wanted to wrestle interpretation from what they saw as the deadening hand of historical criticism. *Truth and Method* was not overtly driven by postmodern philosophy, but it was the catalyst for the development of several different approaches to biblical interpret-ation, some of which are recognizably postmodern (Thiselton, 1992). Postmodernity is not easily defined, and it does not have a clear or coherent central philosophy. This is perhaps precisely because post-modernity is a reaction against the idea that there *is* any coherent and central philosophy that can be used to explain existence. Postmodernity rejects the idea of such 'meta-narratives' and looks instead for meaning that is local, plural and contingent. It is easy to see how such a philosophical background could direct hermeneutics to the preoccupation with real readers that we noted in the previous chapter. Although reader-centred approaches to biblical interpretation have not emerged solely because of postmodern thinking, the latter has certainly helped to promote and justify the move away from the sense that texts have a single, objective meaning that can be understood unambiguously by current-day readers to a sense that texts are opportunities for the creation of meaning by readers. Reading becomes as creative an act as writing (Tompkins, 1980).

Other philosophical currents that have influenced hermeneutics derive from the great thinkers of the nineteenth and twentieth centuries such as Freud, Jung and Marx. One of the characteristics of current approaches to texts is what has been termed a 'hermeneutic of suspicion', the tendency to question the obvious, surface meaning of a text and to ask what may be going on behind the scenes. In psychological terms this implies that texts can be repositories of hidden, unconscious meaning, an idea that draws heavily on philosophies derived from the work of Freud or Jung. In sociological terms the emphasis is on suspicion of the political and social power that creates and uses texts to its own ends, and owes more to Marx than Freud. The 'cultural studies' approach advocated by Fernando Segovia and others (Segovia, 1995) stresses the way in which social forces and expectations can shape the meanings that arise from reading texts. Philosophies that help to expose socially constructed inequalities and oppressions have had a strong influence on hermeneutics generally, and to some extent have found their way into biblical interpretation. Not all of these philosophies sit well with a worldview that accepts the notion of the transcendent, and the possibility of the Bible as the Word of God. It is not surprising, therefore, that the radical deconstruction of the biblical text in order to expose it as nothing more than a reflection of underlying human power structures is not something that many biblical scholars have attempted. Sawing the branch on which you sit is not a wholly sensible hermeneutical strategy. Nonetheless, the philosophical movements that have led to hermeneutical suspicion are important because they show that biblical texts cannot always be taken at face value and that interpreters have a duty to be aware of how they use the power that an authoritative text contains and imparts.

Although postmodernity is an important and pervasive philosophy that has had a widespread impact on hermeneutics, it has not convinced everyone. Some saw Gadamer's apparent abandonment of the author as arbiter of meaning as a dangerous move toward interpretative anarchy. E. D. Hirsch's *Validity in Interpretation* (1967) became a focal point for those who continued to resist unbridled pluralism in biblical interpretation. There are still many biblical interpreters who shy away from the idea that all reading is interpretation and that there is no objective meaning in texts. For them, interpretation requires some sort of evaluation, and a central criterion for such evaluation is what the text might have meant when it was originally written.

The philosophical and methodological developments in hermeneutics have many implications for preachers, and Robert Kysar and Joseph Webb (2006) have produced an interesting analysis of how different ways of reading the Bible might affect preaching. Here we need to highlight two points that are of particular importance for what follows in subsequent chapters. The first concerns the way in which readers have a key role in creating meaning. The second concerns the way in which creating meaning involves different stages or processes. Both points may seem obvious and simple, but sometimes these are the most important points of all.

Readers as creators of meaning

The idea that readers have a key role to play in creating meaning is not new, and has emerged in many different ways and in varying degrees of radicalism in hermeneutical theory. Critics using the historical approach have always been aware of the influence of what they saw as 'reader bias', a problem for those trying to extract the objective truth behind the text. Rudolf Bultmann (1957, reprinted 1985) addressed this problem of 'pre-understanding' (*Vorverständnis*) and understood both the positive and negative sides of reader subjectivity. On the one hand, this subjectivity could cloud the objective truth of the message, shaping it into something that it is not. On the other hand, the gospel message is aimed at subjects, not objects, and it is meaningless unless it encounters the reader and speaks to the reader's context. Bultmann seems to distinguish between individual presuppositions about a text, which he thought could and should be laid aside, and individual experience and 'situatedness', which *are* important if the text is to have any meaningful relationship to the reader. It is here that Bultmann draws on the philosophy of Existentialism by suggesting that a *genuine* life-relation to the text occurs when the subject matter 'also concerns us and is a problem for us'. History comes 'alive' because it is encountered within the context of the reader's own personal history. So, for example, by properly understanding the meaning of the story in Mark 4.35–41 we can make the right connections to analogous events in our lives today.

This perspective is one in which meaning resides in the text, and readers must comprehend that meaning in order to encounter the text correctly. Readers are capable of creating false meanings because they bring with them the baggage of presuppositions, so interpretation requires care and vigilance. Bultmann's conclusion typifies the optimistic belief of his generation that being self-aware of our prejudices and biases is sufficient for us to avoid the pitfalls of our pre-understandings and that the text can still reveal its true meaning.

Others have been much less sanguine about the idea that the text itself contains meaning, and for some this has led to radical views on the role of readers. Stanley Fish represents those who have moved so far away from textual objectivity that the text has all but disappeared when it comes to locating meaning. Fish is a literary critic and professor of law who has a special interest in the poems of John Milton. Originally schooled in the literary criticism associated with structural analysis and formalism, he gradually came to believe that the meanings that he and his colleagues attributed to literary works were not products of the texts themselves, but of readers. His journey away from formalism is described in a collection of essays *Is There a Text in this Class?* (Fish, 1980). For Fish, a text is created only in the act of reading because individual readers create the text according to the expectations and 'interpretive strategies' that they bring to the process.

Fish argued that *all* texts are innately ambiguous and can therefore be interpreted in all sorts of ways. The reason why there are not countless interpretations of given texts, he argued, was because meaning is the product of 'interpretive communities', or guilds of readers who share the same way of constructing and understanding texts. Fish moves meaning away from something objective that is located in the text to something that is the product of a community of readers. In this sense, all meaning is rhetorical: texts mean what we can persuade others they mean. The prevailing interpretation of a text is simply the currently most persuasive rhetorical argument of what the text means, and it is open to being toppled by a more persuasive argument from another interpretative community. Fish's ideas have been roundly attacked for failing to account for the sophistication of language (which is not as inherently ambiguous as he tries to make out) and for slipping into solipsism[1] (Noble, 1994, 1995, 1996; Thiselton, 1992). Nonetheless, the general ideas that readers have a crucial role in creating meaning, and that reading and interpretation are not easily disentangled, are now widely accepted by academic biblical scholars and cannot be ignored by preachers.

One of the reasons why readers may have a key role in shaping the meaning of texts is that they read for different reasons and with different expectations. This is a point made some years ago by Robert Morgan (1988): what you get out of the Bible depends to some extent on what you are trying to do with it. Academic historians are doing one thing whereas readers in churches are doing another. Historians come looking for history and find it whereas believers come looking for the Word of God and not ancient history. Readers may not create meaning but they may select different meanings to suit their purposes. More recently, Stephen Fowl (1998) has suggested that these arguments over meaning are not helpful for reading the Bible in Christian contexts. He promoted the concept of 'underdetermined reading', which bypasses the issue of meaning by concentrating on what people do with texts. This approach accepts that people come to the Bible with different backgrounds and motivations, and tries to take these seriously. The interpretations we give need to be assessed against the motivations and character of those who use the Bible and the effects that their reading has on others. Some might see this sort of ethical approach to reading as the best way of assessing different interpretations, while others would wonder if it still hands too much control from the text to the reading community.

When it comes to assessing the role of readers in creating meaning, most contemporary academic biblical interpreters probably lie somewhere between the naïve optimism of the objective historicists and the radical subjectivity of Fish's anti-foundationalism. Readers are important, but still constrained by the text. The area that seems to be developing most rapidly is interpretation that stresses the importance of the readers and their social location. Socially determined attributes such as gender, race and class are now perceived as key factors that shape the way in which the Bible is understood. Texts may not have an infinite variety of meanings, but they can have different meanings and these differ between men and women, between rich and poor, between developing and developed nations, between clergy and laity, and so on. For many academic interpreters it is quite normal to start an interpretation by highlighting their particular social location and admitting to their particular and limited point of view.

All of these approaches illustrate the importance of readers in shaping interpretation. This notion is almost axiomatic in biblical studies these days, but perhaps it is not always fully understood by preachers. For preachers, this notion relates both to the creation of their message and to the way in which their message is understood by congregations. Before they speak, preachers must read, listen and look. How they 'read' the text, or how they 'read' the congregation, or how they 'read' the times in which they live, will shape the message that emerges when they preach. How that message is understood by others will depend not just on the words that are said, but also on the meanings created by the listeners. Biblical hermeneutics has taken a long and tortuous path to reach what seems now an obvious conclusion, and the journey is probably not over yet. Insofar as preachers need to perceive and interpret messages, they would do well to try to learn from those who have gone before.

Meaning as a staged process

The idea that meaning is created in stages may also seem too obvious to mention, but it is important to recognize and establish that this is indeed so. There are different ways of expressing this idea, which may be partly because different processes are being referred to and partly because more or less the same processes are dealt with in different academic discourses.

The hermeneutical circle is an idea already mentioned, and one that probably dates back to Schleiermacher. It was originally confined to the idea that textual analysis requires knowledge of the general use of language in order to understand the possible meanings of particular texts. However, 'general' use is in reality the sum of particular usage, so the two are intertwined. Each particular use shapes general understanding, which in turn helps to interpret particular use. Schleiermacher also used this idea to link his notions of 'objective' exegesis and psychological 'divination' of the author (Thiselton, 1992). A general grasp of the attitudes or thoughts of the author may help to determine what a particular passage is likely to mean, but the same passage might also lead to a different understanding of the author. These two kinds of information might be appropriated in different ways: the way we perceive or empathize with other people is different from the way we analyse the logic of language.

A second, quite different expression of processes in hermeneutics is to contrast *meaning* and *significance*. This distinction was originally made by E. D. Hirsch (1967), who was reacting against literary analyses that seemed to want to abandon any pursuit of the author's intended meaning. Hirsch viewed this with deep suspicion, and was not convinced that the world of the author was as elusive as many were suggesting. He argued that the author's intent should be the chief criterion for deciding what a text means, though he also accepted that a text could have different significances for various readers. So in our Shipping Forecast analogy, Hirsch would argue that the meaning is what the forecaster at the Meteorological Office wishes to convey; it is the weather being described. The significance of the forecast is the relationship of that meaning to something or somebody. A forecast of winds increasing to 10 or 11 will have a very different significance for someone listening in the comfort of their home compared with someone in a small fishing boat in an area about to be engulfed by the impending storm. Nonetheless, it is the same forecast. In his later work, Hirsch (1976) conceded that meaning could be wider than that which authors intended, so that someone could respond or relate to misunderstood or unintended meaning. However, he still maintained that meaning and significance were two separate entities.

In biblical studies this notion surfaces in the distinction between what the text *meant* and what it *means*. In other words, interpretation is firstly about historical analysis in order to determine what the original author intended and secondly about evaluating what this original meaning says to present-day readers. This idea was famously expressed by Krister Stendahl (1962) in an article on biblical theology, but it underpins a great deal of biblical interpretation in church contexts. This may reflect the way in which historical approaches to biblical studies (which have been around for longest) have spread from the academy and permeated churches (Village, 2007). For some, there is no distinction between these two: the text means now what it always has. Others may accept that the original meaning is accessible, but that it no longer applies today or is applied in a completely different way.

Although many of the more postmodern approaches to hermeneutics would deny this clear separation of meaning and significance, they may nonetheless also involve different processes. Stanley Fish refused to accept the independent existence of texts because he wanted to stress that all reading is interpretation. We do not, he argued, read a text and then decide what it means. To read is to interpret, so meaning is already predetermined. But this presupposes some process that precedes reading, which for Fish is the shaping of minds by the force of rhetoric. The interpretative community (so the story goes) persuades readers to a particular way of reading and this all-pervasive viewpoint channels and restricts the possibilities of meaning that can be understood when a text is read (Fish, 1980). Fish argues that instead of readers perceiving a text and then evaluating it, their evaluation shapes their perception. This may reverse the usual order of things, but it still requires different processes: the community shapes its members, its members shape what they read to produce the texts they understand.

Whatever the different processes involved in interpreting texts, these processes may involve different skills and abilities. With the Shipping Forecast, the original meaning can only be understood if the recipient knows the format of the message and what each particular bit of information means in terms of the weather likely to be encountered in a given place and time. Once the meteorological conditions it describes have passed, a forecast becomes redundant, and the skills employed in decoding that particular forecast are less useful. Those who relate to the Shipping Forecast as 'poetry' may appropriate it in quite different ways that require a more subjective and intuitive appreciation of poetry and imagery.

With the Bible text, there may be good reasons for some suspicion of interpretations that seem to bypass the 'plain sense' of the originally intended meaning. In some instances the original meaning *is* what it means now. However, this is by no means always so, and the original meaning may be utterly irrelevant unless meaning can be drawn from it in creative ways. Preachers who are good at analysing the original meaning of a text may not always be so good at linking what they discover to life today. One of the complaints levelled against historical criticism by churchgoers is that it often seems so preoccupied with discovering what the Bible meant that it never gets around to saying what it means. This might be because these processes require quite different skills.

Conclusion

Modern biblical hermeneutics is very different from what it was 50 years ago, which reflects the currents of change in society at large. The postmodern turn in Western society has influenced the understanding of general hermeneutics, and this has inevitably affected the particular field of biblical hermeneutics. Of the many lessons that can be gleaned from these changes, we have highlighted the growing realization of the importance of readers in shaping meaning, and the fact that handling messages often involves different stages or processes. Although these ideas are understood in different ways, and are not accepted by all interpreters, they are nonetheless core presuppositions that underlie a great deal of modern interpretation.

Preaching is a complex task which interacts with a wide range of disciplines and ideas (see, for example, the range of material in Day, Astley and Francis, 2005). These lessons from hermeneutical theory are important for preachers because reading is prior to preaching, so preachers themselves are involved in the same processes as their listeners. Preachers will need to be aware of how they create meaning, as well as how their listeners are likely to handle what they hear. The lessons are also important because the different stages of creating meaning will draw upon different skills and require different ways of operating. Preachers need to be aware of their own particular preferences and abilities, as well as those of their listeners. In the next chapter we will look more closely at the processes of meaning, and how they might differ between academic and church contexts.

Chapter 3

Perception and Evaluation in Hermeneutics

Introduction

In this chapter we want to suggest that preachers, like their congregations, are 'readers' in the broadest sense: that is, the messages they deliver arise because preachers themselves receive and interpret messages. The processes by which this happens are complex and, as we have seen in the previous chapter, have been described in a variety of ways. However these processes are described, our contention is that they essentially involve the twin processes of perceiving and judging, and that these two processes are at least to some extent independent. Information has to be recognized for what it is and then responded to in some way. In exegetical terms, for example, we might speak of establishing what the text says and then deciding what this means. Others might use terms such as meaning and significance, while yet others may refer to what the text meant then and what it means now. This may seem self-evident, but hermeneutics bids us beware of assuming that the two are that distinct. Before looking at how these processes might operate, it is necessary to establish the case for their independence in the first place.

Relationship of perception and evaluation

We saw in the previous chapter how historical-critical scholars have long been aware that reading and interpretation are not always easy to separate. This difficulty is ascribed to the presuppositions and prejudices that readers bring to the act of reading, and the solution is to foster critical self-awareness. Objectivity for most scholars is the difficult yet necessary goal of good interpretation. For others, this goal has been abandoned because of a suspicion that it is impossible to separate reading and interpretation. Some have completely merged the two by arguing that all reading, indeed all perception, is interpretation. Reading, it is argued, creates meaning by a single process that is governed by what we assume the message to be and what we assume it can say. Although this idea has been pervasive, it has by no means won the day. While most interpreters admit the impossibility of a completely 'objective' reading of texts, they nonetheless believe that texts do have some existence that is independent of readers. For example, Anthony Thiselton (1992) rebuts what he terms radical socio-pragmatism:

> . . . we are offered a false polarization between *either* formalism and old-fashioned liberal impartiality *or* the end of the anti-formalist road in which socio-political conventions swallow up all pretensions to achieve a standpoint outside one's own reading community. But to say, rightly, that no one can fully *reach* the goal of impartiality does not logically entail the proposition that no one can begin to travel down the road toward more critical openness. (Author's italics)

Readers may find it difficult to be self-aware when they read, but it is nonetheless possible to distinguish acts of perception from acts of evaluation. Those who spend their days enveloped in the culture of postmodern academia can sometimes find it easy to overplay the importance of subjectivity and pluralism in hermeneutics. In fact the vast majority of scholarship still proceeds on the basis that writing encodes meaning and that meaning can be shared with others. Those who deny the possibility of identifying the original meaning or intent of authors do not always behave as if this were so. They still purvey their 'readings' of biblical passages through their own texts, presumably on the assumption that they can thereby convey their ideas to readers who will accurately understand them. E. D. Hirsch, a champion of maintaining the author's intent as the arbiter of meaning, recalls that 'I was once told by a theorist who denied the possibility of correct interpretation that I had not interpreted his writings correctly' (Hirsch, 1976).

Although it may be difficult to separate acts of perception from acts of evaluation, these two facets are nonetheless present in most cases when interpretation takes place. The two processes may not operate independently, but they are not necessarily the same thing and both are integral to the overall process by which we create meaning, whatever the context. What then are these processes, and how do they operate in the particular task of preaching?

Processes of perception

The word 'perception' has a variety of meanings that reflect the complexity of the processes it seeks to describe. On the one hand, according to the *Oxford English Dictionary*, it is the 'process of becoming aware or conscious of a thing or things in general'. It is the conscious awareness of the input from our senses. On the other hand, it is also 'a direct recognition of something; an intuitive insight; an understanding . . . an interpretation or impression based upon such an understanding; an opinion or belief'. This last set of definitions shows that perception can be more than the passive logging of sensory information because it is also actively shaped by the mind.

The study of perception has a long history in both philosophy and in psychology. For example, cognitive psychologists have tried to explain the way in which sensory information is filtered to allow us to focus on particular bits of information among the many that constantly bombard us. Early studies of the phenomenon of 'selective attention' (for example, Broadbent, 1958) assumed that unwanted information was filtered out at an early stage, before it could be processed. Such 'bottom-up' models had to be modified in the light of evidence that even information we apparently ignore is nonetheless received and processed by the mind. Increasingly, psychologists are realizing that attention is also controlled by 'top-down' processing that allows previous knowledge and expectations to actively filter sensory input. Several theories have been suggested to explain such 'high order processing' (reviewed by Wells and Matthews, 1994), but no one theory has gained general acceptance. The key point, however, is that even before we are aware of it, sensory information may be filtered and processed by mechanisms that are shaped by our previous experiences, habits or beliefs. We may, as the Bible puts it, 'look, but not perceive, and may indeed listen, but not understand' (Mark 4.11). When we attend to sensory information, the way we attend is controlled by psychological processes.

The second definition of perception reminds us that it can be an insight or recognition of something that may not necessarily involve the senses at all. Perception in this sense is about the connectivity of ideas or information, so that what is being considered is not perceived in isolation, but linked to other ideas or information. Perception can be the process whereby the mind makes links between ideas in such a way as to produce a new perspective or insight. This process might be quite different from the filtering of sensory information and may require a more intuitive approach to handling ideas.

Perception and hermeneutics

If these processes are the innate 'givens' of any act of perception, hermeneutics is, in some sense, awareness that such acts can be deceptive. In the realm of reading the Bible, perception can deceive in several ways. First, it can deceive readers into thinking they have fully or truly discerned the intentions or life-world of the author. In hermeneutical parlance this is to ignore the 'situatedness' of writer and reader, and the horizons of understanding that create the gap between them. In the story of the Stilling of the Storm we can too easily assume that the writer was addressing some universal human condition of fear and anxiety that is symbolized by a tiny boat in a storm-tossed sea. It may be that the author was simply showing that Jesus had divine power over nature in ways that twenty-first-century Western readers find difficult to believe.

Traditionally, one of the first tasks of biblical studies is to draw attention to the gap between the horizons of author and reader, so that students appreciate the effort that is required to bridge it. Those who do not perceive the gap in the first place are likely to have difficulty in understanding what all the fuss is about. Education can help people to realize the complexities of interpreting an ancient text like the Bible, and to develop a healthy awareness of the deceptive power of perception. There is some empirical evidence that Bible readers who have experience of university education, and specifically theological education, are more likely to perceive the separation of horizons when reading a biblical story (Village, 2006).

Second, perception can deceive interpreters into creating literary structures or devices in texts that are more imaginary than real. The fashion for literary biblical study has led to an increasingly sophisticated view of the 'implied author'. One of the criticisms of this sort of reading is that it posits a level of literary competence that could not possibly be ascribed to the original author. It can deceive interpreters into creating meanings and possibilities that are not justified from the text. Education may not be a simple panacea for dealing with the deceptive power of perception because it often creates the 'literary competency' that leads scholarly readers astray. Students armed with an array of literary devices will find all sorts of structures and patterns in a text, some of which are testimony to the creative powers of student readers rather than that of biblical authors. Is the Sea of Galilee really a motif used by Mark to raise the expectations of his readers, or is it just a contingency of the fact that

Jesus was a Galilean who was bound to be on or near the lake at some stage in his ministry in that area?

Third, perception can make readers take very narrow views of a biblical text that are driven by their own preoccupations. If perception is controlled by unconscious processes in higher parts of the brain, then information may be filtered out by the beliefs, prejudices and habits that prevent the text being read in anything other than a very particular way. Information that is trapped by the filter will never reach the conscious brain and cannot therefore be evaluated carefully. This is a neurological explanation of how interpretative communities might so influence readers that they are incapable of understanding texts other than through community norms. Such extreme filtering is very unlikely, but filtering of some kind is almost bound to happen when the Bible is read. Reader-centred approaches to interpretation need to be aware of the power of perception to so reinforce habit that readers find it difficult to see anything other than the familiar in texts. How many readers of the Stilling of the Storm imagine a single boat in storm-tossed waters, totally failing to see the other boats in the flotilla mentioned in the Markan account?

If hermeneutics can make us aware of the problems of perception, it can also show us that the complexity of perception is the prerequisite for a rich and diverse appreciation of texts. Perception allows creativity because it enables different readers to encounter the same text in different ways. Perception that is focused on sensory input will be sensitive to the details of a text and the information it conveys. There may be less filtering, so each piece of information is appreciated and noticed on its own terms. In Mark's account of the Stilling of the Storm, the attentive reader will notice the time of day and coming of night which adds to the sense of foreboding. They may also notice that other boats were in the storm too, or that Jesus was in the stern of the boat and not the bow. Such attentive perception may bring to mind the sounds, sights and smells of what it would have been like to have been in that boat.

On the other hand, perception that is focused on the linking of information and ideas may more quickly grasp the symbolic or metaphorical sides to this story. The physical condition of being in the dark and tossed from side to side in a boat may be easily translated into the sense of uncertainty and rapidly changing mood that can threaten to overwhelm those who are experiencing difficult times of emotional or spiritual instability. The notion of disciples in distress while their master ignores their plight in the storm may be understood as saying something about the general nature of being a disciple when God seems far away. The story may also be perceived in relation to other miracle stories so that the particularities of this event are overlooked in favour of a more general understanding of what is going on. For example, this rebuking of a storm might be linked to the rebuking of demons, showing the power of Jesus over what is seen and what is unseen.

Perceiving is never simply a raw encounter with an object, and the processes that link it to individual preferences, past experience and accumulated knowledge allow texts to be appropriated at different levels and in different ways. To some extent, these processes will be governed by habit, so that readers tend to have a preferred or 'default' way of operating. This does not mean that this is the only way they perceive, and different perceptions can be fostered in different ways. A meditative exercise on the Stilling of the Storm may encourage readers to focus on the details in the text and thereby encounter the story through the senses: seeing the flotilla in the gloom, hearing the wind and the creaking timbers, feeling the stomach-churning lurching of the boat. Those who may more naturally want to skip the details might perceive things in such an exercise that they might otherwise have missed. A brainstorming exercise on the story might throw up a host of creative associations, ideas and questions: the devil in the deep blue sea, Fishermen's Friend, and why does it say 'asleep on *the* cushion' and not 'asleep on *a* cushion'? Those for whom perception is largely a sensory process may gain insights into this story that they would otherwise have missed. Human experience in general, and biblical interpretation in particular, would be a rather dull, single-dimensional affair without the depth created by the complexity of perception.

Processes of evaluation

The term 'evaluation' in this context applies to a broad spectrum of activity that involves some sort of response to what has been perceived. Psychologists have long been interested in how people make decisions, how they respond to choice and how they make more complex moral judgements. In the field of cognitive research there was an early separation between the study of how people make judgements and how they reach decisions.[1] The former looks at the processes used to draw conclusions from knowledge or evidence, while the latter has tended to look at how people choose a particular course of action from among several options. Models of how people make judgements are probably most relevant in this particular context, though judgements and decision-making are clearly related, and in recent years there has been some convergence of theoretical models that seek to explain both processes.

Early approaches to the study of judgement acknowledged that it has a lot in common with perception. In both cases, the brain has to process information from a variety of sources that may be incomplete and falli-ble. In perception, objects are 'constructed' by the mind, which some-times has to estimate the most likely configuration, based on previous experience. Optical illusions are examples of the mind getting it wrong as it tries to construct objects based on incomplete or contradictory information. In the same way, some psychologists argue, judgements are made as the mind appraises the scattered information it receives and tries to form some sort of response that is appropriate to the individual and the particular circumstances. The processes involved may require judgements about what is fact, in which case the mind must be able to predict and estimate from the information it receives, or it may require an evaluation, which implies the action of preferences and opinion.

The relationship between perception and evaluation has been clari-fied by studying the different ways that people make decisions. Humans do, of course, respond automatically to sensory input, and this can be at complex levels. Driving a car involves rapid and complex decisions about what to do next, something that learner-drivers know all too well. Yet these decisions eventually become automatic, so that experienced drivers are no longer aware of dealing with the incoming information, and will often arrive at their destination without any recollection of the multi-tude of decisions they made along the way. By the same token, the complex processes of reading and interpreting can become so familiar that we are unaware of the habits that shape the way we respond to texts. This does not mean that no evaluation is taking place, because the 'norms' or expectations by which we judge things can be applied con-sciously or unconsciously. In both cases, some sort of judgement is being made that will shape the way we understand and respond to what we perceive.

Cognitive psychologists who have studied this distinction between automatic, 'intuitive' decisions and those based on conscious reasoning have assigned them to two different neural systems.[2] Thoughts generated through System 1 (intuition) are more easily accessed than those gener-ated by System 2 (reasoning). System 1 operates quickly, automatically and effortlessly, whereas System 2 operates more slowly and requires more conscious effort. Decisions made through intuition are often emotionally charged, governed by habit and therefore less open to control than the consciously monitored, deliberately controlled and reasoned decisions of System 2 (Kahneman, 2003). Reasoned decisions may be applied using some sort of rule-based system, though these rules are not applied automatically, so there is often room for flexibility. In terms of the way it operates, System 1 is more akin to the automatic operations of sensory perception: the difference is that perception operates on sensory information whereas System 1 works on conceptual ideas. In many ways this cognitive psychological model includes the distinction noted earlier between the two definitions of perception: one based on perceiving sensory input, the other being insight and linking of ideas. In the evaluation model, System 1 corresponds to the latter sort of perception, suggesting that some sorts of perception and some sorts of evaluation are difficult to separate.

In the context of hermeneutical evaluation, cognitive psychological models indicate that some decisions about meaning may be driven by semi-automatic processes that are hard to recognize and difficult to control, whereas other decisions require the more conscious application of hermeneutical 'rules' or method. This does not necessarily mean that reasoning is better than intuition because intuition may become more accurate with experience. Experts can often arrive at the correct solution quickly and without consciously thinking about the problem. This is because evaluation that was initially done by conscious thinking has become semi-automatic, and moved from System 2 to System 1. The expert appears to 'perceive' the solution as soon as they perceive the problem, whereas novices have to rely on a step-by-step conscious working out of the problem. We may therefore not be aware of how we evaluate, especially if we are making decisions about routine matters that we encounter often.

Many psychological notions of judgement are based on the idea of weighing input against a norm or set of criteria. Theorists have produced a number of different models that explain how experts and non-experts make decisions. One such theory, image theory, suggests that people narrow the options they might choose by assessing them against three 'images' that contain their values and morals, their goals and aspirations and their strategies for attaining their goals (Beach, 1998; Galotti, 2007). Image theory suggests that the way people approach decisions when they have a number of options is to narrow down those options by rejecting those that do not fit the various images they have. In this 'screening' phase, any options that violate the various images are excluded, so that only those that are compatible with images reach the stage of choosing between options.

Although there has yet been no study of how this might work in terms of reading the Bible, there are some clear links with the suggestion that what readers get from a text depends to some extent on what they are reading it for and how they are reading it. The values and morals image in this context will include beliefs about the nature of scripture and what subjects the Bible can or cannot address. If this is so, it may explain why some readers reject different interpretations of a text almost automatically because they violate images of what a 'proper' interpretation should be. Only those that meet a certain set of criteria are likely to be given serious consideration. If this is so, then it is important that readers are aware of the origin and nature of the particular images they are using as norms because such images will have a powerful influence on how they read.

Evaluation and hermeneutics

If these various psychological processes are an innate part of evaluation, hermeneutics is, in some sense, awareness of the sometimes arbitrary nature of the way we decide what something means. A central preoccupation of biblical hermeneutics has been to try and establish the validity, or otherwise, of different criteria by which texts are judged. Most scholars of hermeneutics have long accepted the fact that deciding if an interpretation is 'true' requires an answer to the prior, and biblically famous, question 'What is truth?' Hermeneutics has not necessarily brought the answer any closer to contemporary academics, but it has made them self-consciously aware that deciding between a 'true' or 'false' interpretation can only happen within a particular framework of shared understanding. Academics may be trained to resist the 'automatic' filtering that cuts down evaluative choices, but as experts they are still likely to operate within a particular set of acceptable criteria.

So, for example, academics might offer different 'readings' of Mark 4.35–41 to their peers, and the value of these readings would be judged according to the particular discourse in which it is located. Douglas Geyer (2002) compares a range of written sources that preceded this story in an attempt to demonstrate how it would have been understood at the time. Part of his argument is based on an analysis of the Greek word used in verse 39 for 'sea' (*thalassa*) and he draws on ancient myths that refer to gods calming the sea in order to show that Jesus' actions would have been widely understood as demonstrating divine power. Historicists will judge whether the Gospel writer could have been deliberately drawing on pre-existing stories and ideas, and, if so, whether they would have been understood in the way that Geyer suggests. The evaluation relies on deciding how accurately the historical sources have been interpreted and how widely read they might have been in the first century.

Geyer also sets the Stilling of the Storm in a wider narrative framework which he terms a 'cycle of uncertainty', running from 4.35 to 6.56, and which he believes helps to interpret the Gospel as a whole. This is a literary interpretation based on the assumption that the key to understanding the Gospel of Mark is the crucifixion, an event of unexplained horror. Geyer (2002, p. 4) argues that the juxtaposition of blessing and violence, safety and terror, certainty and uncertainty in the death of Jesus is the final and supreme example of what he calls the 'anomalous frightful event'. The Stilling of the Storm is the first example of this sort of event in the narrative, and begins the cycle of uncertainty. A key justification for this interpretation is the final reaction of the disciples, which is fear caused by uncertainty of who this powerful person is. Geyer argues that the story ends with this reaction (rather than a reaction of joy at being saved from drowning) because the narrator is introducing the idea of the anomalous frightful event and so preparing the reader for the crucifixion. Formalist literary critics will judge whether this perceived literary structure is genuinely there in the text or just the creation of the critic. To do this they must decide how likely it is that the text could have been constructed in such a way, and whether the Stilling of the Storm is likely to have been understood by the author of the Gospel as linked in this way to the crucifixion.

The above example shows how historical or literary critics might employ different evaluative criteria to a particular interpretation. As we have seen, some academics are much more reluctant to evaluate in this way, believing that there are no 'right' or 'wrong' readings, just different readings from different people in different circumstances. However, there are limits to this interpretative generosity, and even those who believe meanings are entirely the product of readers will question the validity of those readings that are abusive or ethically dubious. In general, then, evaluation operates at the level of weighing the validity of a particular perception of the text against the agreed criteria of the academic discourse in which the scholar operates.

It might seem that this awareness of the complexity of judging interpretations marks out academic approaches to reading the Bible from those practised in the Church. However, this is not so, and Adam (2006) points out that the Church has always employed rational criteria for evaluating interpretations, even though these are varied and sometimes ill-defined. In theological readings of the Bible, the interpretation of any given text has to be judged against the wider 'meta-narrative' of the Christian gospel as a whole. In other words, interpretations may be judged less by how well they cohere to the particular text and more by how well they cohere to some overall understanding of what the faith is all about. A 'true' interpretation is one that conforms to the nature and purposes of God; a 'false' interpretation may be one that subverts that view by imposing human misunderstanding on the text. Deciding the nature and purposes of God is difficult and contentious, so evaluations are generally against the nature and purposes of God as understood within a particular religious tradition. The 'Nice sermon' comment at the church door can often mean 'Glad to see that you believe what I believe.' Silence (for few people tell preachers that their sermon was bad) may betoken disinterest, or a sermon that fell short of the mark as judged by the theology of the listener.

Conclusion

This chapter has highlighted two key components of the hermeneutical process: perception and evaluation. We have argued that although these are linked in many ways, they are not the same thing. Hermeneutists have debated this point and, although opinion is divided, there remains a strong body of opinion that accepts the notion that different perceptions of the text can be evaluated against the shared criteria of a particular discourse. Psychological insights of perception and evaluation show how they may be linked and how they operate at conscious and unconscious levels. It is inevitable that these processes will often go on unnoticed, so that we are not always aware of the limits of our perception or the criteria by which we evaluate. This 'automation' enables minds to handle routine tasks more easily, which is why experienced experts find it easier to make decisions than do inexperienced novices. This is equally true for preaching, where seasoned preachers generally spend less time, and have less anxiety, in creating sermons than do those who have just begun their ministry. Preachers would have short careers if every sermon was as tortuous and difficult as their first. Nonetheless, the familiarity of experience needs to be examined periodically so that preachers are aware of the processes by which they create and deliver their messages.

Preachers, then, need to be aware of how they and their listeners perceive texts and sermons. What information is 'filtered out' so that it is never noticed? What are the expectations or habits that will shape ambiguous information in such a way that it appears to be unambiguous and familiar? Is this perception that attends to the sensory information available, or is it a more intuitive perception of insights about ideas? Preachers also need to be aware of how they and their listeners evaluate sermons. Is a sermon 'good' if it interprets a text in a way that conforms to expectations and supports the status quo? Is it good if it fosters harmony and charity in the hearts of those who hear it? Is it good if it stirs up anger, embarrassment and dissent? Do we take a pragmatic view and argue that it is good if it achieves something concrete that makes a difference to the real world? Or can it be good if it does no more than fire the imagination and stir the heart for a few moments?

The processes of perception and evaluation are integral to all areas of hermeneutics, not just the reading of written texts. 'Unwritten texts' may seem to be a contradiction, but remind us that messages are encoded in many forms including visual and aural. Broadening the definition further, 'text' might include the sub-texts and 'agendas' of society or congregations, the material of cultural studies and discourse analysis. Reading the signs of the times is no less important for preaching than reading a learned commentary on a lectionary text. All these various 'texts' will, to a greater or lesser extent, shape the messages that preachers create. The next three chapters look more specifically at how the processes of perception and evaluation operate when preachers read the Bible, the Holy Spirit and the contexts in which they preach.

Chapter 4

Reading the Bible

Introduction

Psychological models of perception and evaluation have not, generally, interacted with the world of academic hermeneutics, nor with the world of church-based Bible reading and preaching. This may be because the empirical nature of much cognitive research in these areas requires that constructs be simplified and therefore made rather artificial. Theories are often constructed or tested using stylized information presented to classes of willing, or not so willing, undergraduates. Nonetheless, the processes of perception and evaluation are important in a wide range of contexts, and not least in the task of preaching. To illustrate this point, this chapter will focus on interpreting the Bible, which is an important component of preaching. The aim is to show how different ways of reading the Bible in church contexts involve the processes of perception and evaluation.

The way in which the processes of perception and evaluation operate when someone interprets the Bible will depend to a large extent on how they approach the task in the first place. Anthony Thiselton (1992) ends his review of biblical hermeneutics *New Horizons in Hermeneutics* by proposing a number of different ways of reading texts, each of which is linked to particular hermeneutical theory and directed toward a particular 'reading situation'. The following examples illustrate some of the perceptive and evaluative tasks in five of these reading strategies.

Reconstructionist reading

According to Thiselton, Reconstructionist reading tries to understand the world and intentions of the author, accepting that some texts have a very definite 'direction' of meaning that resists the attempts of readers to impose their own meaning on them (Thiselton, 1992). This sort of historical approach requires readers to reconstruct the world of the author because this is understood to be indispensable to the meaning of the text. Reconstructionist reading owes a great deal to Schleiermacher and, as such, it is not simply a detached rational process. As mentioned earlier, it may also involve a more intuitive 'divination' of meaning which counters the inadequacy of using rationality alone by using the imagination to create a picture of the author. As pictures of what the author was trying to convey emerge, they are evaluated and refined in order to achieve the best understanding possible. This cycle of perception and evaluation against the evidence is the core of the hermeneutical process in this type of reading.

Although some readers may stop when they consider that they have understood the author as much as they are able, preachers will need to go beyond this by making some response to the message thus uncovered. Is it a message that has value? Is it still directly applicable today, or must it somehow be translated to make it significant to congregations? In this sense, there are different levels of evaluation: the first relates to evaluating how accurately the author's intent has been identified, the other is a broader evaluation of what that intent means in a different context. This is what Hirsch called the significance of a text rather than its meaning.

A Reconstructionist reading of Mark 4.35–41 may come to very different conclusions depending on how the passage is perceived and evaluated. If it is perceived as an accurate account of what happened, then the details of the story will be noted as the recollections of those caught up in an extraordinary event. The author's intent is to be an accurate witness, or an accurate recorder of testimony, so getting the facts right will be important to establishing the veracity of the story. The evaluation of the story is then likely to centre on the demonstration of Jesus displaying miraculous power over nature, and what this says about his nature, or about the way God operates in creation today. Preaching that is based on this sort of reading will probably need at some point to tackle the difficult issue of what it means to ask God to change natural forces today.

A Reconstructionist reading, however, does not necessarily need to be a literalist one, because the passage could equally be perceived as a fictional story created by the author for a particular reason. The details in the story might then be understood as devices used by the author to convey an image or idea. For example, the story is set at night to increase the sense of foreboding and the sea is 'rebuked' to convey the image of demonic forces being subdued. If this story is perceived as being created by Mark to help first-century Christians, then the reactions of the disciples to a frightening storm may be interpreted as analogous to the reactions of Mark's intended readers who were facing different sorts of calamity at the time. Evaluation of this perceived intent is likely to focus on what Mark wanted to convey about Jesus or discipleship through the use of this story. Preaching that is based on this sort of reading is likely to explore what it teaches present-day disciples about faith and trust in God.

Existentialist reading

Existentialist reading stresses the impact of the text on the individual. Thiselton (1992, p. 563) suggests that this approach appeals especially to those who prefer to do their own individual reflection, and for whom the 'shared habits, practices and expectations of the reading-community somehow ring hollow'. In this sort of reading, the text calls for decision and response, and requires the active involvement of the reader. Rudolf Bultmann drew heavily on Existentialism in order to avoid what he perceived as the deadening effects of historicism that sought only what the text meant and not what it means, thereby leaving the task of interpretation half done (Thiselton, 1992). In this sort of reading, the perception of the text is more interior and intuitive because readers have both to understand the message and to relate it to their own lives. More evaluative judgements may have to be suspended in order to permit the message to stir the individual into a direct response.

For some preachers, this sort of reading might suggest that their prime task is to proclaim the Word, rather than interpret it for their listeners. Thomas Long (1989) points out that this is one important way of understanding preaching, and one which portrays the preacher as 'herald' of the gospel. In some traditions there is a positive aversion to moving from the indicative (what the text says or promises) to the imperative (how the text is applied) because the latter is considered to be the work of God directly in the lives of those who hear the message (Carrick, 2002). This does not mean that there are no interpretative processes involved in handling scripture in this sort of reading, even if some exponents think otherwise. The text must be established, reiterated and exposited, and this requires perception and understanding, even if the message itself undergoes rather little evaluation. The challenging thrust of the message has to be perceived and translated into language that will enable the hearer truly to encounter the original intention of the proclamation. This, after all, was the reason why Rudolf Bultmann (1985) attempted to 'demythologize' the Bible: not to explain it away, but to make the encounter between Word and hearer more likely in the modern world. How this is done will depend on how preachers themselves perceive and evaluate the fundamental message of the gospel.

An Existentialist reading of Mark 4.35–41 might perceive this story as a challenge for disciples to deepen their faithful expectation of God. It might, therefore, place the reader in the boat in order to explore what is happening to the disciples. These are fishermen, completely familiar with this lake and its propensity for sudden squalls. They know these boats and they know how to handle them in rough seas. Yet this is something different, something beyond their understanding and control. In the midst of the everyday and the familiar they are suddenly confronted by their fragility, mortality and vulnerability. This is a crisis moment in the lives of these followers of Jesus. Their response is to awaken Jesus, but only to complain about his indifference. They have not even the faith or grace to plead for help from the one who can save them. No wonder they are awestruck at the end, when this Jesus has acted beyond their wildest expectations.

Evaluation of this kind of reading is likely to ask how much it mirrors human reactions to crises and whether a petulant but utterly honest outburst to God is sometimes the only authentic response. Preaching that is based on this sort of reading might need to explore what things constitute 'storms' in the lives of the listeners, and how they are stilled. This direct interpretation might be counter-productive for some for whom the careful and powerful exposition of being in the boat in the storm is sufficient in itself to produce an Existentialist encounter with the text. Some listeners do not want preachers to do too much.

Narrative reading

There are many different ways in which the Bible may be read as narrative, and Thiselton makes several links between Narrative theory and reading in pastoral situations. A common feature is the way in which readers are drawn imaginatively into the narrative world of the text and thereby transformed. This transformation may be by projecting future possibilities, by forming or confirming expectations, by subverting convention or by allowing a better appreciation of people and personhood.

Thomas Long (1989) points out that one way of understanding preaching is to see it as storytelling, and this way of preaching is becoming increasingly popular.

Again, it could be argued that this approach to preaching requires rather little in the way of hermeneutical process apart from re-telling the story. If this were true, Bible readings would suffice without the need for sermons. Re-telling a story is not necessarily the same as simply reading it from the page, and preachers need to enable their listeners to hear it as if for the first time. Re-telling a story can involve careful attention to detail so that things that might be overlooked are brought to the forefront. Re-telling a story often means translating it into new settings so that it can speak in a fresh way. In particular, biblical stories that were originally shocking and subversive can, by dint of familiarity, lose their cutting edge (Village, 2006). Recreating them in unexpected ways can preserve the message as it might have been intended originally. These processes require preachers to be able to inhabit the narrative of the text, to comprehend the message and to translate that message into another narrative world. Even if the original story is left unchanged, narrative preaching has to tell the story in ways that allow listeners to engage with insight and understanding. Narrative preachers must have empathy both with the characters in the story and with their listeners.

A Narrative reading of Mark 4.35–41 might pick up on the motif of the sea and the rich biblical imagery associated with it: the waters of chaos in Genesis; the sea parted to bring slaves to freedom; the waters subdued by the command of God; the sea calmed by offering Jonah to the deep. The imagery of the storm with its arbitrary violence, confusion and noise might be contrasted with the strange pool of stillness surrounding Jesus asleep on the cushion in the stern. The calmness and control of Jesus could be contrasted with the angry frenzy of the disciples. Or perhaps the story could be set in the wider context of Mark's Gospel using the disciples' reaction of awestruck terror as a narrative link to the Markan resurrection story.

Preaching that is based on Narrative exposition will concentrate on bringing the story to life and allowing it to do its own work. I have seen this passage preached in an all-age service for the families of ordinands about to start their training at theological college. Volunteers squatted on the floor and joined hands to make the boat, sheets made the sea, and a couple of families made up the storm-tossed crew. Amidst all the fun and laughter, the passage spoke powerfully to people caught up in one of those life transitions where we find ourselves well beyond our comfort zones. The parallels between the story and the lives of those ordinands and their families hardly needed to be made.

As with Existentialist reading, the emphasis of a sermon based on Narrative reading may be on perception rather than evaluation. Nonetheless, the preacher will need to do evaluative work in preparing a re-worked narrative. Most stories are rich and multilayered, and can be told in several ways from different points of view. Some recent films and books have explicitly used repeated or parallel telling of a story from different standpoints as a narrative device. Preachers will usually want to take a particular standpoint on a narrative for a sermon, and must decide which it is to be and why. Telling the Stilling of the Storm from the viewpoint of the disciples will not be the same as telling it from the viewpoint of Jesus, which is different again from the detached viewpoint of someone in one of the other boats. The preacher's job is to perceive the possibilities of these various viewpoints and to decide which is best suited to a particular occasion.

Spiritual reading and biblical symbols

A fourth type of reading that Thiselton identifies is associated with image, symbol and metaphor. He refers to the work of Paul Ricoeur and Paul Tillich who drew respectively on Freud and Jung to explore biblical symbolism. Ricoeur, for example, noted the fact that symbols are open to many possible meanings, and this can lead to both positive and negative outcomes. The negative outcomes relate to the way in which symbols can serve the self-interests of readers because they allow the projection of self-will and self-deception. We can interpret symbols to suit our own ends. The positive side is the possibility of creative imagination that re-shapes and re-creates symbols to have new meanings. These two aspects of reading biblical symbols suggest the need for readers to draw on different psychological processes. Avoiding the negative use of symbols requires critical processes that evaluate the way we use them. Preachers sometimes need to be iconoclastic in order to break the power of abusive religious symbolism. Encouraging the positive use of symbols requires the free play of creative imagination. Preachers sometimes need to be whimsical in order to encourage congregations to find greater depth and power in the symbols on which they rely.

Some preachers may decide that biblical symbol and metaphor speak for themselves; others may decide that symbols used in one culture can be dangerous and hurtful if unleashed uncritically on people of another culture. Preaching requires a fine balance of processes if symbols are to be used helpfully. With too much creative play, symbols become putty in our hands, vulnerable to misuse and abuse. With too much analysis and evaluation, symbols are explained away and lose their essential power.

Symbolic reading of Mark 4.35–41 has obvious links to those mentioned earlier which use the story as an analogy for life or discipleship. If the passage is perceived as a metaphor for the life of the Church, a reading that focuses specifically on symbolism might explore the boat and its relationship to the sea. The boat is not alone (for other boats were crossing with this one), but there is a sense of isolation. The sea once calm and benevolent is suddenly furious and hostile, threatening to sink the boat. This is powerful symbolism for the Church that is sometimes so at home in society yet sometimes the object of persecution. The world can seem a Godless and malevolent place looked at from inside the Church, which can see the world as threatening its very existence. Yet God rules both Church and world. This perception of the passage as symbolic in this sort of way needs evaluation because it has important implications. If the boat is the Church, is Christ confined to it? Is this symbolism creating harmful dichotomies between the Church and world, the saved and the lost, the haves and the have-nots?

Preaching that is based on Symbolic reading might point to the symbolism in the passage, but let the listeners draw their own conclusions about what it means. Or it might specifically follow the implications and point out the useful and the dangerous connotations that can be carried by these symbols. This is a passage that lends itself to metaphorical interpretation, but such interpretations are open to conscious or unconscious manipulation. The lessons of psychology may be particularly important in this context for helping readers and preachers understand that intuitive and reflexive evaluations of symbols are not always the best.

Reader response

We noted in Chapter 1 that the current fashion for reader-centred interpretation of the Bible in academic circles has arisen independently among literary critics, postmodernists and ideological critics. Thiselton (1992) suggests several ways in which reader-response theory might help Bible reading in pastoral situations. He draws attention to a well-used analogy with performing music: just as a musical score is the basis of many performances, each of them unique and depending on who is performing the piece, so the Bible text is the basis for each unique 'reading performance' that depends on the particular context in which it is read and who is reading it. Stanley Fish's (1980) radical assertion that texts contain no meaning that is independent of readers may seem rather unfruitful material for preachers. After all, nearly all would want to ascribe to the Bible some divine revelation that is not simply the product of human minds. However, Thiselton argues that at the very least a radical reader-response approach draws attention to the unconscious assumptions that pervade every reading community, and that can easily be assumed to be universal truths, rather than local tradition.

Preachers may sometimes step into a minefield by inadvertently violating local assumptions, especially when invited to preach outside their particular faith tradition. Some might shape their message to their listeners in order to avoid upset. There is no point, they may argue, in preaching a liberal sermon to fundamentalists or vice versa. Others might see this as the best way to stir people out of their cosy assumptions. Reader-response theory sheds light on both the merits and drawbacks of these two tactics. Stepping too far outside a community's expectations may be self-defeating because listeners will simply not be able to make any sense of what they are hearing. Meaning arises not just from what preachers say, but also from the expectations and experience of listeners that allow what is heard to be understood. However, reader-response theory also reminds us that the Bible must sometimes be freed from the mollifying tendencies of communities which blunt the challenge of the unfamiliar by interpreting it into something that is recognized, familiar and safe. Sometimes it is good to make people encounter something that they cannot at first understand. When Moses saw the burning bush (Exodus 3.1–6), he had no categories by which to understand what it was, but the encounter was one that fired his curiosity and changed his life.

Preaching that is based on a reader-response interpretation of the Stilling of the Storm might deliberately draw attention to the assumptions or expectations that particular congregations bring to the story. In a situation of social comfort and wealth, the stress may be on challenging the easy assumption of God's benevolence. Is this story a panacea that tells us that God will always bring peace and calm into the storms of our lives? Do we imagine ourselves as the faithful ones who have no fear because we trust our Saviour? Or are we the smug ones who can rest assured only because we have never watched the waters of chaos and death spill over into the heart of our lives? In a congregation full of despair and gloom, the stress might be on challenging the assumption of

God's incapacity. Are we so focused on the storm that we cannot see the one sleeping in the stern? How long will we frantically try and bail out the boat before we turn to the one who can truly save us? Do we simply repeat the disciples' mistakes or learn from them? Reader-response approaches are not shy of taking two apparently contradictory sets of meaning from the same text. The particular circumstances of individual congregations require preachers to respond to the Bible with an enlightened flexibility that allows passages to remain powerful and relevant to a wide range of listeners.

Conclusion

Thiselton describes several other ways of reading the Bible in pastoral contexts, but the above examples are sufficient to show that all readings require the application of different skills and processes. In some ways there are strong links between these various ways of reading the Bible: Existentialist encounter can be encouraged by a range of other sorts of readings, Symbolic reading is often linked to storytelling and Reconstructionist reading can involve examining narrative in detail. Nonetheless these are different ways of reading that may well lead to different ways of preaching, as we have suggested. The common requirement for those who read with a view to preaching is to perceive the various possibilities offered by a text and to decide which offers the most appropriate message for a particular congregation at a particular time. Each message will itself need to be carefully scrutinized to ensure that it coheres with the text and with a wider understanding of the Christian meta-narrative.

The field of biblical hermeneutics has generated many different ways of approaching texts, many of which are appropriate for preachers. The various types of reading described in this chapter might be used by different preachers, by the same preacher on different texts or by the same preacher using the same text on different occasions. Approaching biblical texts in particular ways will lead to particular sorts of interpretations. This is not the same as saying there are no 'right' or 'wrong' interpretations of the Bible. We have shown how each type of reading has its own emphasis on the processes of perception and evaluation, with some readings being stronger on perceiving than on evaluating. Even where the emphasis of a sermon is on perception, the preacher is still required to do evaluative work so that the congregation is not misled or abused by what is preached. Although some preachers may argue that the Bible speaks for itself, and preaching is merely the reiteration of what is already on the page, this is not so. If it were, 'preaching' would be confined to the public reading of scripture for those who were unable to read it for themselves. Bible-based preaching always selects and shapes the messages of scripture, and preachers need to do this with honesty, openness and self-understanding.

Just how this happens may be driven partly by prior theological convictions, but also by preferences and habits. Some will prefer to analyse texts carefully, reading them in their own terms and paying attention to detail. They will be wordsmiths who treat each word carefully and will not lightly change them for modern terms or new translations for fear of exchanging well-tried and familiar truths for passing fancy. Others will concentrate on ideas behind the words, and will perceive texts in relation to a wider flow of ideas that may go beyond the obviously religious. Words convey ideas, and ideas are linked in ways that create new ideas and new words. Those who have a more intuitive perception of texts may be more inclined to liberate ideas from the words that contain them, enabling a more creative and playful interaction.

Evaluating texts may also involve different preferences and habits. To a large extent these evaluations are likely to be theologically driven, so that texts that conform to prior beliefs are more likely to be used by preachers than are those texts that challenge or disrupt that belief. However, the worth of a particular text might also be judged by a wider range of cognitive or emotional processes operating at a more unconscious level. For some preachers the test of a good message is whether it coheres, makes rational sense and illustrates clear principles. Whether it upsets the congregation is neither here nor there: if it is true it should be preached. For such preachers it is vital to speak the truth in love. For others, good messages are those that are good for the listeners. They will be drawn to messages that build up congregations, increase unity and strengthen faith. Texts that are confrontational or disruptive may be avoided, even if what they say is true. For such preachers, all things may be lawful, but not all are expedient.

One reason why preaching is never the simple reiteration of the biblical text is because preachers also use other sources for their messages. The requirement for preachers to engage with the biblical texts through a combination of perception and evaluation can be applied to other areas that impinge on the creation of messages. The next two chapters look at how hermeneutics applies more widely to non-textual 'reading' that is relevant to preaching.

Chapter 5

Reading the Spirit

Introduction

The previous chapter explored the roles of perception and evaluation in the particular context of reading the Bible. This chapter expands that exploration to include other arenas in which these processes may be important for preachers. Hermeneutics has often concentrated on the interpretation of texts, and in the context of preaching it is easy to assume that hermeneutics applies only to how the Bible is read and interpreted and how its messages are transmitted to others. However, hermeneutics is about meaning in general, and meaning derives from a wide range of sources. Reading is not confined to texts: we read the times in which we live, we read people, we read congregations and we read ourselves. These uses of the word 'read' remind us that the processes of perception and evaluation are constantly being applied to the people and objects that surround us and that non-verbal meaning plays a crucial part in shaping theology (Adam, 2006). Preachers have the particular task of bringing these various contexts together and allowing them to interact with each other. It is out of this interaction, out of these various readings, that preachers shape their messages.

The Christian tradition has long recognized, but struggled with, the role of the Holy Spirit in shaping meaning. A written text is more tractable than something as ephemeral and untrammelled as spirit, so it is not surprising that academic writers have tended to steer clear of the subject. The same has been said of those who teach homiletics, though Greg Heisler's recent book *Spirit-led Preaching* (Heisler, 2007) is a lively rallying call to allow the Holy Spirit to drive preaching. Such calls tend to eschew what is perceived as the 'modern' trend for dry textual exposition, psychological mumbo-jumbo or lame, pastorally based preaching in favour of allowing the Holy Spirit to infuse every part of the process of discerning and delivering sermons. To be sure, any theology that takes the Trinity seriously has to account for the action of God in inspiring and guiding preachers, but to argue for spiritual inspiration of preaching in such broad terms pushes back the question of how this operates in practice, and often leaves it unanswered. Discussions on the way in which Bible, Holy Spirit and expositors interact have a long and complex history and are not the subject of this chapter. Instead we aim at a more limited objective of exploring what it might mean in terms of perception and evaluation for preachers to 'read the Spirit'.

Reading the Spirit in the Church

Insofar as God's interaction with creation is through the Holy Spirit, discerning the Spirit's presence, action and intent must surely lie at the heart of preaching. In this sense, reading the Spirit is an over-arching category that summarizes the entire work of preaching. There is, however, a more specific understanding of what reading the Spirit means, which stems from the need to respond to those who claim spiritual gifting or insight and who wish to lead others in a particular direction. This may or may not be overtly charismatic behaviour, and could be as mundane as someone suggesting a particular course of action for a congregation. Preachers may be required to speak to these situations, and this requires them to interpret what is going on and to discern the divine within it. Sometimes the message seems to be contrary to what is traditionally understood to be the will of God, and such cases require careful perception and evaluation.

This process of 'reading the Spirit' is evident in scripture itself, particularly in the fledgling Church at a time before there were many specifically Christian texts available. The churches founded or overseen by the apostle Paul consisted of people who had responded to the message of salvation in Jesus Christ. Those who were Jews would be familiar with various religious texts, but gentile Christians had only remembered and recounted teaching or a handful of apostolic letters to guide them. In Galatians, Paul seems to be addressing people who were finding it difficult to anchor their new-found faith in practical morality and everyday ethics. Faced with uncertainty, they were tempted to adopt the rules and regulations of the Jewish scriptures as a more concrete way of discerning the will of God.[1]

Paul's anxiety and response is driven by his belief that reverting to the written code subverts the new relationship to God, a relationship which is founded on the indwelling Christ and trust in the Spirit. In a famous passage, Paul lists the fruits of the Spirit (Galatians 5.22–23) and argues that his readers should be able to trust their spiritual instincts when it comes to discerning the good fruit from the 'works of the flesh'. Given the wayward effects of 'trusting to the Spirit' at Corinth, this is a bold step. The spiritual excesses referred to in the Corinthian correspondence show how difficult it can be to read the Spirit. It is easy to become so pre-occupied with the experience of a spiritual encounter that we lose sight of its purpose. So Paul reminds those caught in spiritual excess that the purpose of spiritual encounter is the building up of the community of faith (1 Corinthians 12.7, 14.26), and that the ultimate expression of the Spirit is love (1 Corinthians 13) rather than charismatic gifting.

The need to 'test the spirits' (1 John 4.1) is inevitably part of the role of the preacher. This applies at many levels, but is perhaps most urgent where contemporary culture collides with tradition in ways that force the Church to discern and decide. When novel ideas challenge established practice it is often preachers who must read the Spirit: is this God doing a new thing to which we must respond, or is this sinful humanity kicking against the traces? In recent years, churches have been confronted with a host of changes that one group or another claims to be the fresh wind of the Spirit. Whether it is dealing with the spiritual enthusiasm of the Toronto Blessing or the moral conundrums created by changing views on sexuality, preachers may need to decide what the Spirit is saying to the Church.

Luke Johnson (1996) uses the story of Peter and Cornelius (Acts 10.1, 11.18) as a model of how churches can discern the work of the Spirit. When Peter is confronted with clear evidence that gentiles have been filled with the Holy Spirit he is forced to rethink the boundaries of what constitutes the people of God. The evidence appeared to contradict the received wisdom of scripture and tradition because gentiles, considered beyond the reach of God, seemed to be genuinely encountering God through the Holy Spirit. The narrative suggests that Peter read this movement of the Spirit correctly, but others needed to be convinced (Acts 11.1–18). Although there was an initial acceptance that this was genuinely of God, the issue was debated a second time at the Council of Jerusalem (Acts 15), and even after this second debate the matter seems to have continued to cause the kind of divisions that prompted the Letter to the Galatians. Eventually, those previously considered beyond the boundary were accepted as being part of the people of God, and discernment of the activity of the Spirit had enabled the scriptures to be read in a new light.

This is not a process confined to history. Stephen Fowl (1998) drew on the work of Luke Johnson (1996) to suggest that evidence of the Spirit-filled lives of practising gay Christians may allow churches to accept them as bona fide members and therefore reach a new under- standing of the bounds of acceptable sexual practice. His point is primarily that, if being Spirit-filled was accepted as a legitimate criterion on which to judge the lives of practising homosexuals (and he is not sure that it is), it could only be applied if there was contact between hetero- sexual and homosexual Christians. The Spirit is manifest in people, so reading the Spirit requires contact with people: it was Peter's willingness to go to Cornelius' house that began the process of change.

Deciding upon the validity of major shifts in doctrinal understanding is not the prerogative of many, but preachers may be required to respond to specific words, events or actions that some congregation members claim are 'Spirit led'. Within the Pentecostal and Charismatic traditions, the action of the Spirit is closely associated with the expression of particular charismatic gifts such as speaking in tongues or prophecies. These explicit claims that God speaks through the Spirit have to be set alongside more widespread implicit claims that arise when people begin to act in ways that they believe to be divinely inspired, but which seem to fly in the face of received wisdom or traditional practice. These situa- tions require both the ability to perceive and evaluate what God is doing among congregations.

Hermeneutical and psychological insights can help to reinforce theo- logical understandings of what it means to read the Spirit, and so suggest good practice for preachers. The hermeneutical suspicion that it is diffi- cult to perceive without interpreting, and the psychological evidence of powerful high-level filters that control perception, suggest that it is not easy to be open to the Spirit. Perceiving the Spirit may be hard for preachers who rely heavily on the evidence of physical senses and on well-tried patterns of prayer and liturgy. The Spirit by nature is difficult to pin down: 'The wind blows where it chooses, and you hear the sound of it but you do not know where it comes from and where it goes. So it is with everyone who is born of the Spirit' (John 3.8). Those who prefer the routine, safe and familiar patterns of religious life will find it difficult to perceive the work of God outside the particular confines of what they are used to. The filtering can be so strong that contrary information is never really noticed or accepted. In the Parable of the Sower (Mark

4.3–4), Jesus speaks of seed that falls on the path and is eaten by birds before it even sprouts. Could this be an analogy for those who do not respond to the Spirit because they never perceive the Spirit?

Those who give the Spirit a narrow remit will tend to treat novel or unusual beliefs or behaviours with suspicion and label them as ungodly or foolish. The tendency to overlook the divine because it is novel is not confined to non-charismatic traditionalists, because even in 'Spirit-led' churches there are customs of behaviour and shared expectations of what constitutes the work of God. Pentecostal and Charismatic traditions have their own particular manifestations of the Spirit and these can be routines that are rigid and ritualized. Those outside these traditions will have different ways of understanding the work of the Spirit, but these may also be tightly prescribed. The point is that for most people in a given tradition there will be an acceptable and recognized way in which God is assumed to be present with people. Preachers need to maintain openness to perceiving the action of God in both familiar and novel ways across a range of circumstances. Sometimes this requires a critical awareness of the way in which perception blinkers us to the unusual or the unfamiliar.

Those whose perception tends to be more intuitive may be more open to novel ways in which the Spirit may operate, but this too carries dangers. We noted in an earlier discussion of evaluation how psychologists have identified the 'System 1' level of decision-making that operates at an unconscious level and that is similar to the unconscious filtering of perception. At this level, perception and evaluation may not be distinct, so that intuition makes reflexive judgements on what is observed. This leads us to make our minds up about something before we have fully understood it or appreciated it for what it really is. Intuitive perception can easily jump to wrong conclusions.

In the Gospel of Mark, Jesus performs many exorcisms in the early part of his ministry (Mark 1.23–26, 34; 3.11; 5.1–13). Those who opposed Jesus did so because they could not accept his violations of religious norms and taboos: the forgiving of sins (Mark 2.1–12), the breaking of Sabbath rules (Mark 2.23–28; 3.1–6) and the flouting of purity laws (Mark 2.16). It seems likely that this challenge to tradition led to mounting anger and frustration among those for whom ritual obedience was central to their understanding of faith. These emotions seemed to shape powerfully the way in which Jesus' ministry was perceived and evaluated. There was no suggestion that his exorcisms were faked, so another explanation was necessary: 'He has Beelzebul, and by the ruler of demons he casts out demons' (Mark 3.22). Here is the same phenomenon being seen in two completely different lights: some see the working of the Spirit of God, some see the working of Satan. The inability to see the action of the Spirit for what it truly is may have stemmed not so much from a reasoned, considered evaluation but from the kind of intuitive decision-making that operates at the unconscious level and is often emotionally charged.

Preachers today need to be aware that God moves in mysterious ways. To read the Spirit means first being open to the Spirit, and therefore open to the possibility of encountering God in the novel and the unfamiliar. Spiritual encounters need to be experienced in their own terms, without linking them too quickly to other experiences or other ideas, and without allowing the reflex of habit to interpret meaning. Sometimes we need to resist our natural perceptive tendencies in order to make room for spiritual experience.

This is not to say that such experience should not be judged, and both scripture and experience suggest that it is very unwise to accept every such act and utterance as a manifestation from God. Paul tells the Thessalonians not to 'quench the Spirit' but nonetheless to 'test everything' (1 Thessalonians 4.19–21). Some of the problems highlighted by the Corinthian correspondence seem to have arisen because the Church found it difficult to distinguish true words of prophecy from false ones. This may have prompted Paul to write, 'I want you to understand that no one speaking by the Spirit of God ever says "Let Jesus be cursed!" and no one can say "Jesus is Lord" except by the Holy Spirit' (1 Corinthians 12.3). This suggests an evaluation that is based not on the mode of delivery, but on the content. Similarly, in the Letter to the Galatians 5.22–23, Paul argues that the operation of the Spirit is evidenced by the content of that action, the 'fruits' of love, joy, peace and so on. Paul clearly encouraged his churches to live by the guidance of the Spirit, and an integral part of this was to evaluate spiritual experience in order to sift the genuine from the false.

This process of evaluation requires the conscious and reasoned examination of the evidence. This is not necessarily the application of detached logic to the phenomenon, for this would elevate human reason above the mind of God. Evaluation at this level may require a measure of how much following this path would increase the kind of love and harmony mentioned by Paul in 1 Corinthians 13 as the goal of spiritual life. Those best able to evaluate this may not be people who prefer to make judgements on purely rational grounds. On the other hand, the heated emotional atmosphere of some spiritual encounters may require just that sort of critical analysis that is not easily swayed by current fashion or the need to please. What price a cool head in the middle of spiritual nonsense? Given the range of different sorts of evaluation that are required, it seems sensible to make decisions corporately, and this seems to be what the early Church did.

Preachers need to read the Spirit if they are to discern the movement of God in their particular context. This requires the ability to resist the filtering and narrowing tendencies of perception in order to ensure that the potential presence of God is not overlooked or too easily rejected through habit. It also requires the careful and conscious application of judgement so that congregations can avoid the perils of being easily misled on the one hand and stubbornly unmoved on the other. Preachers have a role in interpreting the Spirit for and with the people, and this is a hermeneutical task.

Reading the Spirit in the secular

Alongside the requirement of preachers to read the Spirit in specifically church contexts is the parallel requirement to read the movement of the Spirit in society at large. The interaction of the Christian community with the world shapes, and is shaped by, its understanding of the Bible and the Church (Watson, 1994). For some, the Spirit acts narrowly within the Church and through scripture. For others, divine inspiration is to be found in all sorts of places, some of them very far from the obviously sacred. A broad view of the work of the Holy Spirit implies that there are ideas, messages and inspiration woven through the discourses and narratives of secular society that reveal something of the nature and action of God. If this is true, then there are 'texts' of many different types that preachers must attend to in order to discern what the Spirit is saying to the Church.

Texts are presented through a wide range of media today, and go well beyond the kind of text you are reading now. Culture is increasingly encapsulated in books, films, television, web pages and hypertext. Literacy broadly conceived links preachers to a wider community of ideas, both within and beyond the Christian faith. Preachers must be scribes of the kingdom, sifting through cultural narratives to find treasures that are old and new (Matthew 13.52). The aim of this section is to explore how perception and evaluation affect the hermeneutical task of reading the Spirit in the texts of our times.

Hermeneutics shows how our preconceptions of what a text is or is not can shape the meanings that are likely to be gleaned from it. For some theorists such as Stanley Fish (1980) this is such a powerful force that the meanings available to readers are wholly confined by their expectations of what a particular text is and what it could mean. These expectations are created by interpretative communities that use the power of rhetoric to persuade their members that this, and this alone, is what the text means. The evidence for an overriding influence of interpretative communities in church contexts is mixed (Village, 2007), but the idea that our prior commitments may shape what we consider a text to be (and therefore what it can or cannot mean) is important when looking for the Spirit in the secular. Preachers generally belong to a particular ecclesiastical tradition, and the mores of that tradition are likely to influence the boundaries of what are considered legitimate texts on which to base sermons. Is it possible for God to speak through texts other than the Bible, including wholly secular ones? For some this might seem a silly question because they will perceive plenty of material for sermons in 'secular' literature, and much that points directly to God. For some, a sermon can be based just as well on a poem or a newspaper article as on the Bible. For others, preaching is expounding the Bible and only the Bible: other literature might be helpful if it stems from the Bible, but most 'human' ideas are irrelevant at best and downright dangerous at worst. These two caricatures highlight the way in which prior assumptions about the nature of texts determine what they can mean.

In theological terms this is a question of revelation, and specifically the nature of the Bible in relation to other sources of truth about God. Prior beliefs about the nature of scripture are likely to be a powerful filter that will decide how it and other texts are read. Beliefs about the nature of the Bible vary widely, but there is a broad consensus that, in one way or another, it brings authoritative revelation of God. Such a high view of scripture creates the necessary impetus to allow detailed analysis of every part of the text, and the justification for finding theological consistency across very different sorts of writings within the canon of scripture. Without some sense of the uniqueness and reliability of scripture, the whole enterprise of detailed textual analysis and theologically driven biblical interpretation threatens to disintegrate. It is the prior assumption of divine revelation (however that is understood) that drives and shapes the hermeneutical task of engaging with the Bible, and this assumption must underpin all preaching.

The corollary of such a view of scripture can be a low view of other literature as a source of divine inspiration. Strongly conservative views of scripture assign to it a unique *and exclusive* role in revealing God. Theologies that deny the possibility of God speaking through the secular are likely to create mindsets that are suspicious of the output of unbelievers, those of other faiths or even those within the same faith. More liberal views of scripture downplay its uniqueness, and therefore open up the possibility of finding divine revelation in other texts. In this view, the possibility of human error in the Bible militates against too close a reading, and inspired messages from other sources may be more valuable than the apparently ungodly message of some parts of scripture. Extra-biblical texts will be read not just to 'see what's going on out there', but to 'hear what God is saying out there'. The challenge is to know how to evaluate the messages that the world has to offer.

These prior beliefs and understandings will tend to shape the possibilities that are perceived from a particular source and how it is evaluated. At this level, perception will operate to filter texts to a greater or lesser extent, and preachers need to be aware that this is happening. Those who deny the possibility of divine revelation beyond the Bible will never perceive it, even if it is there. Those who are open to divine messages from anywhere may perceive them everywhere, and be unable to tell the genuine from the false. The ideal hermeneutical strategy is to be open to the full range of divine revelation while at the same time being alert to the possibility of counterfeit.

Insight into how tricky it can be to strike the balance comes in the form of an analogy from a story in the Gospel of John. When Philip tells Nathanael that he has found the Messiah and it is Jesus from Nazareth (John 1.43–51), Nathanael's immediate response is, 'Can anything good come out of Nazareth?' Whether this was an informed question based on an understanding that the Messiah would come from the line of David (and therefore from Bethlehem not Nazareth), or a less than generous comment on the type of people who lived in Nazareth, Nathanael's scepticism is evident. Nazareth is not the place in which to go looking for God. To his credit, this is a question rather than a statement, and he accepts Philip's invitation to 'Come and see.' Jesus seems to know this man Nathanael, and sums him up immediately as 'an Israelite in whom there is no deceit'. Nathanael is taken aback by this and startled that Jesus seems to have seen him sitting under a fig tree. Overwhelmed by this apparently supernatural insight, he undergoes an extraordinary change of mind: 'Rabbi, you are the Son of God! You are the King of Israel!' Nathanael's rather touching naïvety in accepting Jesus so quickly on such thin evidence points to a gullibility that perhaps requires some correction. Jesus tells him that he will see firmer evidence on which to make a judgement: 'You will see greater things than these.'

Laying aside the possible reasons why the author of the Gospel may have included this story in his narrative, this is an interesting account of perception and evaluation. Nathanael's rapid move from undue scepticism to undue optimism highlights how difficult it can be to deal with the possible presence of God in unlikely sources. Preachers may need to be as innocent as doves and crafty as serpents when it comes to reading the Spirit in secular texts: openness to revelation from new sources must be combined with healthy hermeneutical suspicion.

Conclusion

Rounded preaching must engage with the written word of the biblical text and the contemporary revelation of God through the Holy Spirit. Clearly the two are intimately linked, though we have not rehearsed the theological arguments that might describe and justify such a link. Our focus has been to emphasize that reading the Spirit is a hermeneutical task that shares common underlying processes with reading the Bible: that is, the need to perceive and evaluate. The substance of perception in this case is much wider and less easy to describe because it covers all the extra-biblical activity of God in creation. As with belief about the Bible, perceiving God acting in creation is a matter of faith and tradition, and some will be more willing to do so than others. This is particularly true of the work of the Spirit beyond the Church, where it is difficult to separate the profane from the sacred.

Reading the Spirit requires self-awareness and self-control. Although there is important theological truth in saying that the Holy Spirit underwrites the whole act of preaching, this is not the same as saying that all preaching is 'of the Spirit'. It is dangerous to assume that 'Spirit-led' preaching is that which is accompanied by 'inspiration', 'power' and obvious positive response from the audience, while anything else lacks the divine imprint. This can too easily drive preaching into a narrow emotionalism that limits and perverts the possibilities of true revelation. Self-awareness implies the ability of preachers to understand how they perceive the action of the Spirit, and why they are likely to accept some manifestations and reject others. Such awareness may confirm that natural or learned habits do indeed allow the Spirit to be heard, or they may suggest the need for a more open mind. Self-control implies the ability to evaluate what is heard, so that preachers do not become prey to every whim of fancy or fashion. Not preaching one of your good ideas can be the best thing for your congregation if it is little more than another of your good ideas.

This chapter has moved the hermeneutical issue from the biblical text to the wider 'text' which is the revelation of God beyond the Bible. The focus has been on how preachers might hear and respond to the voice of God in the activity of the people of God and in the theatre of creation. Sometimes these arenas need to be examined in their own right for the equally important task of discerning what God is *not* doing and *not* saying in order to bring the transforming Word of God into a particular context. This is the prophetic task of reading the times, and it is to this that we turn next.

Chapter 6

Reading the Context

Introduction

There is a strong tradition in preaching that sees its prime task as speaking to, and speaking for, the needs of the congregation. Thomas Long (1989) refers to the 'preacher as pastor' in his typology, and this way of conceiving the task became particularly important in some churches during the twentieth century (see, for example, Ramsey, 2005). Although the idea of preaching as individual or group therapy is less important than it once was, the notion of the sermon as a key instrument for promoting care in congregations remains as strong as ever (see, for example, Allen, 2004; Pagitt, 2005; Ramsey, 2005; Smith, 2004). If sermons emerge from, or are directed toward, a particular group of people, then preachers must be able to 'read' those people: that is, to discern their thoughts, attitudes, emotions or needs and to understand the social and religious contexts they inhabit. If this seems to be pandering to modern (or postmodern) tastes it is worth remembering that this awareness of context is the core of the Old Testament prophetic tradition. It is precisely because the prophets knew the people and understood the political and social contexts in which they lived that they were able to deliver such incisive and powerful messages. Whatever else may have inspired and guided them, it was a passionate engagement with a particular context that drew from them the warnings and encouragements that they claimed were the oracles of God.

The ability to contextualize sermons is an essential component to all preaching. Even where preaching is considered to be the text-driven proclamation of the gospel, the effectiveness of each particular delivery will depend on its relevance and timeliness for the listeners. An evangelistic sermon that calls people to take up the Christian faith may be unnecessarily confusing and disorientating if it is delivered to those who have been Christians for some time. A sermon aimed at encouraging faithful believers will miss the mark if it is delivered at a wedding where hardly anyone who is present is a practising Christian. It might be argued that God is capable of using sermons in all sorts of ways, and there are doubtless examples of apparently inappropriate sermons transforming people in unexpected ways. But this is no basis for a regular preaching ministry, and those who preach week by week in the same place, as well as those with a more itinerant ministry, need to be constantly aware of the contexts in which they operate. Once again, we want to argue that perception and evaluation are key processes in reading contexts.

The contexts of preaching

Preaching takes place in a number of contexts, many of which overlap. The primary context in which most sermons are delivered is a local church congregation. This might be described in terms of its sociological characteristics: its age profile, sex ratio, class structure, ethnicity and so on. These social characteristics are broad categories that give a rough indication of the kinds of experiences and worldviews of the congregation. Such categorization does not allow for the particular history of a congregation, nor the uniqueness of each individual within it, but it should not be dismissed as irrelevant. Social context is a way of referring to common features that link some or all of a congregation, and the shared understandings that arise from this are bound to affect the way in which sermons are interpreted and understood. Preachers who know their congregations will be aware of whether the sociological profile provides useful information to guide the shaping of sermons, or if particular local circumstances mean that first appearances are deceptive. Social location is now seen as a key factor that influences interpretation and meaning, and preachers need to have this sort of insight into their congregations.

Theologically, church congregations are local manifestations of the Body of Christ. The Pauline image is used to emphasize the interrelatedness of worshippers (Romans 12.4–5; 1 Corinthians 12.12–13, 26–27), their individuality (Romans 12.6–8; 1 Corinthians 12.14–20, 27–31), their equality before God (1 Corinthians 12.21–26) and the use of gifts for the good of others (1 Corinthians 12.7, 14.12). Preaching in the context of the Body of Christ is preaching with the knowledge that this is one ministry among many, given to individuals for the building up of

God's people. The metaphor of the body prescribes limits on preachers that should prevent them imagining that they have a superior position in this exchange. If the Body of Christ is the fundamental context in which sermons are produced and delivered, then preaching will have to bring Word and Spirit into meaningful interaction with the people who constitute that body. No matter how challenging or confrontational the message, the end result must be the 'building up' of the people of God (1 Corinthians 14.4; 1 Thessalonians 5.11).

Preaching to church congregations is also set in a particular liturgical context, which will be important in forming meaning for those who hear sermons. Whatever the particular tradition and pattern of liturgy, it surrounds the sermon and shapes the expectations and impact of the preaching event. A sermon in a typical Anglican communion service is set in the Ministry of the Word, which precedes the Ministry of the Sacrament. Lectionary readings often centre on a theme that is reinforced by the words of the Collect. So before the preacher even begins, threads of meaning are being woven in the minds of the congregation. Connections have been made between texts, and this may continue after the sermon as the liturgy moves on to the creed, peace, prayers and communion. The regular gathering of people for sacred service recalls and enacts the fundamentals of their faith. Sermons that emerge in this context form a particular genre of spoken utterance that carries its own implicit meanings and expectations. Preachers must use this genre, sometimes relying on shared meaning, sometimes subverting expectations, and to do so requires them to understand the particular liturgical context in which they operate.

Not all preaching is in the liturgical context of the regular weekly worship of the people of God. Preaching is also proclamation to unbelievers, and this might happen in very different sorts of contexts. Sermons may not be the method of choice for evangelists these days, but messages must nonetheless be shaped, delivered and received. Preachers operating outside the familiar environment of church-based liturgical preaching need to be aware of the context and how this will shape the expectations of listeners. The street preacher with a loudhailer and a placard saying 'The wages of sin is death' has already sent a powerful message to passers-by, a message that is probably not the one intended. The same message delivered to the preacher's congregation on Sunday would probably be instantly recognized and reassuringly familiar. Effective evangelists have long accepted the need to read carefully the contexts in which they operate.

Whatever the general context of a sermon, there will often be a particular pastoral context in which it is delivered. Thomas Long (1989) points out that the trend for preaching to the particular 'felt-needs' of a congregation has grown in popularity, but is rejected by those who believe that the primary impetus for a sermon's message must arise from the Bible. Pastoral context could include a wide range of issues that preoccupy people listening to sermons. Whether preachers choose to ignore these or not, they are still there and will still influence the way in which listeners understand what preachers say. Congregations that are preoccupied with a particular tragedy or a particular joy or a particular threat will find it strange if preachers do not address the issue in some way. Hermeneutics shows how readers and listeners shape meaning, and it is likely that what preachers say will be understood in relation to preoccupying issues, whether they are directly mentioned or not. At an individual level, personal circumstances will often cause listeners to draw from sermons unintended messages and meanings. As we have seen, hermeneutical theory explains and legitimizes this sort of activity. Preachers cannot ignore the pastoral contexts in which they preach: like it or not, this context will influence how messages are handled and interpreted.

The individual or corporate lives of listeners are not the only contexts for a given sermon. There is also the context of the preacher. Preachers bring to their ministry their own history, preferences, skills and experiences. They bring to a particular sermon the situation in which it is conceived and delivered. Again, some would argue that preachers are irrelevant to proclamation of the Word, and too much self-attention is counter-productive. It is certainly true that preachers should not allow self-occupation to overshadow the task: they are not delivering *their* gospel, and self-awareness does not, of itself, produce good preachers. Nonetheless, it is naïve to think that preachers are the anonymous apparatus that delivers the messages of God. Preachers are not radio sets, whose performance depends simply on being tuned to the correct divine frequency. Just as the Bible is the product of interactions between humans and divine agency, so are sermons the result of complex interactions between preachers, their world and their God. Preachers are part and parcel of the context of preaching.

Reading people and congregations

Jesus seems to have had an extraordinary ability to understand the lives of those around him, which enabled his words to connect directly to their particular circumstances. The ways in which he engages with the Samaritan woman at the well (John 4.1–26), Zacchaeus (Luke 19.1–10) and the rich man (Mark 10.17–22) show how he could read their lives and understand their inner fears, anxieties and needs. He clearly understood the strengths and weaknesses of his disciples, and could predict their actions and reactions. Whether this was a miraculous ability, or the gifted application of human faculties, is not clear. There are occasions when Jesus seems to be surprised by people he meets, such as the centurion in Luke 7.1–10 and the Syrophoenician woman in Mark 7.24–30. Nonetheless, the Gospel writers agree that Jesus understood people: he was able to read their characters and their lives, and this was an important aspect of his ministry.

The ability to 'read people' in the context of preaching is the ability to perceive their worldview and engage with it effectively. This is not a new idea: several writers concerned with the communication of the gospel have pointed out how Paul adjusts his message at the Areopagus in Athens (Acts 17.16–34) to suit his audience of Greek philosophers (Flemming, 2002; Losie, 2004). For preachers, this kind of reading may partly be about having the time and inclination to get to know their listeners, and partly about how that knowledge is processed and applied. When it comes to reading people, the processes of perception and evaluation will depend on how preachers engage with congregations. Some preachers will find it easy to interact with people, and will immerse themselves in the lives of individual congregational members or groups. Others will be more detached, and may find it easier to observe from a distance. For some, evaluation comes only through engagement and empathy; for others, evaluation requires a distancing that allows people to be understood in more objective terms. However it is done, true reading of people often requires us to go beyond the surface appearances and discern what is happening at deeper levels. Superficial engagement can lead to false perceptions and poor judgements.

Pastoral models of preaching stress the need for preachers to interact with their listeners, so that preaching is a dialogue or conversation between preacher and congregation. This need not mean an actual dialogue during the delivery of the sermon (though this can be done), but rather an ongoing conversation between preacher and congregation that results in sermons that are dialogical in nature (Allen, 2004). As with any dialogue, the ability to communicate a relevant and meaningful message depends on understanding the shared conventions and expectations that govern the genres of this discourse. This kind of understanding is most likely to emerge when preachers are part of the community that they address. Social engagement with congregations is important for preaching, but some preachers may find this easier than others.

Reading congregations requires the ability to perceive both their local particularity and their location in a wider social setting. Preachers who can *only* understand the local situation are unlikely to be able to bring the objective discernment that enables congregations to be challenged and changed. Being able to perceive a particular congregation in relation to others enables local traditions and peculiarities to be properly understood and evaluated. Perceiving a congregation in its wider social or historical settings is the precursor to being able to discern properly what God might be doing with it or saying to it. How do the traditions and practices of members of congregations relate to the society to which they belong? Are these people poor and vulnerable, or are they idle and callous? Are they rooted in the surrounding neighbourhood, or cut off from it? Do they succumb to fashion or resist change? The ability to read people requires attention to detail and a wider appreciation of the bigger picture.

When it comes to perceiving congregations there is once again a tension between careful observation and wider contextualization. The former requires getting to know people as individuals, observing their lives, listening to their stories, sharing their emotions. The latter requires a wider perspective, linking one person's story to another, making connections to wider trends in the community or society, analysing what has happened and seeing what might happen in the future. These are different skills, and different preachers may find they prefer one to the other. For some, contact with people will be the inspiring material for sermons, and pastoral visits will do more to shape a sermon than any amount of Bible study. For others, individual stories will mean little unless they are linked to a wider flow of ideas and to the context of the whole congregation. Details of individual lives will be less stimulating than the general sense of history or purpose: strategic planning and new initiatives will fire the imagination and provide material for sermons.

Perceiving the setting, aspirations and needs of a congregation is not an end in itself. If this were true, the role of preaching would be reduced to speaking *for* them, but not *to* them. Pastoral models of preaching have been criticized because preachers may end up telling congregations only what they want to hear. The writer of 2 Timothy may have had this in mind: 'For the time is coming when people will not put up with sound doctrine, but having itching ears, they will accumulate for themselves teachers to suit their own desires' (2 Timothy 4.3). This means that alongside perception of congregations must also be some kind of evaluation that enables the preached word to be relevant and transforming. Some may find the idea of preachers 'judging' people distasteful and inappropriate, with the implication of a holier-than-thou preacher pouring judgement and damnation from the pulpit. Evaluation is not about condemnation, but about the important process of deciding what this particular group of people needs to hear on this particular occasion.

Reading social, political and cultural contexts

Jesus called his followers to be salt to the earth and light to the world (Matthew 5.13–14). Two key tasks of preaching are to interpret faith to the world and interpret the world to the faithful. Apologetic preaching goes back to the origins of Christianity, as does the task of explicating the significance of the secular world for the Church. Each of these is an enormous topic in its own right, and it is not our intention to show how to preach in these different contexts. Our more limited aim is to point out that all preaching takes place in social, political and cultural contexts, and that hermeneutical competence requires preachers to be aware of how these contexts shape meaning. This sort of reading has links to what was said in the previous chapter about reading the Spirit in the secular world. In this section we look at the secular, not as a source of divine revelation, but as a context in its own right. In biblical terms, 'the world' is often used to refer to those outside the household of faith and as such it is sometimes couched in negative terms. Yet the world forms both the context and the purpose of preaching, just as love for the world was the context and purpose for the coming of Christ (John 3.16). Preachers both operate in, and serve, the world beyond the congregation, and understanding that world is part of their task.

We have already pointed out the growing interest in how the social location of readers shapes their perception of biblical texts (see, for example, King, 1996; Segovia and Tolbert, 1995a, 1995b; Sugirtharajah, 1995, 2001). For many interpreters, context is the overriding interpretative key because it defines the purposes and goals of reading. Feminist interpreters look for readings that address the issues of women today. Liberationist interpreters look for readings that address social and political injustices, and that offer hope for the poor and oppressed. The strength of such methods is that they allow texts and sermons to relate to issues of real importance in contemporary society. The weakness lies in the ease with which partisan preoccupations can be paraded as divine dictate. Effective preaching requires serious engagement with society, culture and politics, and an equally serious attempt to ensure that the integrity of the gospel is not compromised by that engagement. Socio-pragmatic approaches to hermeneutics, which give precedence to the reader's context over the content of texts, might suggest that compromise is unavoidable because meaning is impossible without it. This is not necessarily so: the secular context may be the milieu in which preaching happens, but it can itself be understood through the processes of perception and evaluation.

Reading the contexts involves a great deal of selectivity and attention. There is simply too much information available to allow preachers to perceive and react to everything. Reading in the sense we have used it here is about discerning what is important, relevant and crucial to shaping the task of preachers and the content of sermons. If perception is selective, then it is important that preachers understand how and why they attend to particular aspects of the secular world. Are they drawn to fact and information, or are they ignited by ideas and concepts? Is politics the down-to-earth art of the possible, or the driver of aspiration and vision? Is the world a comfortable, optimistic place, or an alien place of Godless humanity? Perception of the world is complex and often linked to habitual and unconscious ways of sifting what we see around us.

To some extent these perceptions are governed by different theological stances that may be consciously or unconsciously used to evaluate culture. The notion of being 'in the world but not of the world' runs through the Judaeo-Christian tradition, and is exemplified by those stories that portray the people of God as being supported through trials and tribulations inflicted by a corrupt and fallen world (Noah's ark, the Exodus and the book of Revelation, to mention a few). Alongside this negative understanding of the world is a more positive appreciation of the original goodness of creation. This tradition is exemplified by stories of the creative and sustaining activities of God and counter-cultural voices in the Bible that find Godliness beyond the bounds of Israel. These different perceptions of the world are not mutually exclusive, and there are many instances in which they interact and survive in tension. Preachers who read the world must hold in tension the goodness of God's creation and the seriousness of the fall. Preachers whose reading of the world is unduly negative may be unable or unwilling to address the important concerns of listeners. Preachers who readily engage with secular contexts need to ensure that these do not become the sole agenda of sermons.

Evaluating the world is, however, shaped by more than beliefs. Our innate preferences may also determine how we weigh the events of life. Some may react by responding subjectively to the impact, rather than objectifying it. Reading the world is sometimes about understanding what it is like to be in someone else's shoes. When a disaster strikes, what makes it so are not the bare facts but the tragedy of lives lost or lives changed for ever. Are the teenagers who binge drink just another symptom of a social trend, or unique individuals with their own reasons for doing what they do? Others may evaluate situations using facts and principles. For them, the seriousness of a particular tragedy depends on how many people are affected and the cost to society. The importance of attitudes or beliefs depends on how common they are or what they are, and not who holds them. Individual cases are significant mainly as evidence of wider trends and principles that must be weighed and critically analysed. Again these are not mutually exclusive ways of perceiving or evaluating the world, but particular preachers may tend to use one or the other. What society or culture or politics 'means' will depend to some extent on how we engage with these areas and how we evaluate what we see.

Conclusion

We have tried to show that the messages that preachers create emerge from the complex processes of reading, whether this is reading the biblical text, the Holy Spirit, the Church or the world at large. These different reading contexts are not isolated from one another, but always overlap in any particular person. The processes of reading are a combination of perception and evaluation that together allow preachers to create their messages. These processes are shaped by prior beliefs, experiences and preferences, which are brought to bear on whatever particular information is being read or observed. The study of hermeneutics shows that meaning is not simply objective truth that can be packaged and passed on intact from preacher to listeners. Before they speak, preachers must read, listen and observe, and the way they go about this will inevitably shape the messages they produce. In hermeneutical parlance, meaning arises out of the interaction of texts and readers. For preachers, texts are more than written texts, and a wide range of sources will feed into sermons.

We have noted the ways in which the same biblical story, the Stilling of the Storm, can be read in different ways. Different preachers who start with the same biblical text will end up with different sermons, and the same preacher may produce a different sermon from the same text on different occasions. This variation is partly because of the particular contexts and circumstances in which preachers operate, but also because preachers are unique individuals. They have their own ways of operating and their own preferences in reading. In particular, the way they perceive and evaluate the various 'texts' that give rise to their sermons will vary from one preacher to another.

Sermons are the distillation of reading by a particular preacher. Preachers who were readers are now authors and transmitters of texts. They create new texts that are then delivered to 'readers', the people who listen to preaching. Congregations are 'readers' who receive messages, so what has been said about preachers as readers also applies to congregations as listeners. They bring with them beliefs, experiences and preferences that will shape how what is said is heard and how what is heard is understood. Again, the processes of perception and evaluation will be important, and these will vary from person to person.

Those who work in the field of general hermeneutics, as well as those whose interest is more specifically about interpreting the Bible, have come to see that individual differences play a crucial role in shaping the understanding of messages. Even those who rightly affirm the possibility of accurately identifying and objectively evaluating intended meanings would still concede that the reader has an active and important role in the hermeneutical process. Preachers have a complex role in the preaching discourse because they are readers who must create messages that they themselves transmit. In some sense they embody author, text and reader. Understanding the way in which the particular characteristics of preachers will affect the task of preaching is therefore crucial to helping people preach effectively. Such an understanding will benefit from models of individual differences that can shed light on how preachers create and transmit their messages, and how those messages are received and understood by congregations. The remainder of this book examines preaching in the light of the notion of individual differences in order to see how this may shape preachers and preaching.

Part 2

Preaching and
Psychological Type

Chapter 7

Theology and Individual Differences

Introduction

In the first part of this book we invited our readers to join us on a journey through the field of hermeneutics in general and biblical hermeneutics in particular. The journey has been important for two reasons. First, the journey has reminded us that, as preachers, we are each and individually involved in an interpretative process when we engage with biblical text and when we 'read' that text through our own uniquely shaped perspectives. Second, the journey has reminded us that, as preachers, we have a responsibility to be aware of the variety of engagements with that same text which may be evident among those with whom we are sharing our ministry of preaching. If we take hermeneutical theory seriously, we become even more aware of our responsibility as preachers to listen as well as to proclaim. If we take hermeneutical theory seriously, we accept our responsibility not only to read the text, but also to read the Spirit within the Church and within the secular world, and to read the context within the congregation and within the wider community.

The aim of the second part of this book is to draw on psychological theory to help us to engage in these tasks more deliberately and more effectively. In Part 1 we have inevitably drawn on psychological theory as such theory has impinged on specific aspects of the debate concerning hermeneutics. In Part 2, however, the focus changes and psychological theory comes to the forefront of our agenda. We are not unaware, however, that using psychological theory in this context can be controversial. We need to prepare the way, therefore, by identifying the *theological* grounds for engaging with psychology in this manner. Moreover, we are by no means alone in emphasizing the relevance of psychology for biblical hermeneutics.

Against this background, the present chapter introduces the second half of our book by discussing three issues. First, we examine the wider interest in psychological biblical criticism as this sub-discipline of biblical hermeneutics became consolidated in the early 1990s. We undertake this review of psychological biblical criticism in order to locate our theory within a broader context. Second, we examine the theological significance of the way in which we employ the notion of personality. We undertake this theological examination in order to establish the location of our understanding of 'personality' within the major themes of Christian doctrine: creation, fall, redemption and sanctification. Third, we take care to establish a clear and biblically grounded distinction between two terms that are often (and unhelpfully) confused: personality and character. This discussion helps to clarify further the theological import of the way in which we are employing the idea of personality in the rest of our book.

Psychological biblical criticism

Wayne G. Rollins and D. Andrew Kille are two North American scholars who have done much to draw together and to focus the disparate initiatives which they have come to describe as 'psychological biblical criticism'. In one of their most recent books, *Psychological Insights into the Bible: Texts and Readings*, Rollins and Kille (2007) trace the antecedents of this approach back to pioneering works in the mid-nineteenth century and early twentieth century. They draw particular attention to two works: *A System of Biblical Psychology* by Franz J. Delitzsch (1867) and *The Psychology of the New Testament* by M. Scott Fletcher (1912).

Recognition of the re-emergence of psychological biblical criticism in the late twentieth century was marked in 1991 by the formation of the Psychology and Biblical Studies programme unit of the Society of Biblical Literature. This unit has now matured into a fully established Section of the Society of Biblical Literature. This psychologically informed sub-discipline of biblical studies has come of age.

In the clear and perceptive preface to their reader, Rollins and Kille (2007, pp. xvi–xvii) identified four key factors that contributed to the re-emergence of psychological biblical criticism during the late twentieth century. First, Rollins and Kille point to 'change within Western culture', whereby the concepts of modern psychology have become embedded within the ways in which ordinary men and women reflect on and speak about their everyday experiences. In their analysis Rollins and Kille observe that 'everyone from bankers to novelists, artists, theologians, and cab drivers found themselves speaking with a psychological accent' (p. xvi). It would be very strange indeed if such a cultural shift left untouched the ways in which the study of biblical literature were undertaken.

Second, Rollins and Kille point to 'change within the field of psychology'. Psychology as a discipline is not now what it might have been thought to be in the middle decades of the twentieth century. Much of modern psychology is now once again more sympathetic toward religion in ways reminiscent of trends in the early days of psychology. Early studies in the psychology of religion include classic texts like William James' (1902) *The Varieties of Religious Experience* and G. Stanley Hall's (1917) *Jesus, the Christ in the Light of Psychology*. An expert review of modern developments in the empirical psychology of religion is provided by Spilka, Hood, Hunsberger and Gorsuch (2003) in the third edition of their text *The Psychology of Religion: An Empirical Approach*. Moreover, the developing literature in the field is being stimulated and fostered by a range of specialist journals including *Archive for the Psychology of Religion*, *International Journal for the Psychology of Religion*, *Journal of Psychology and Christianity*, *Journal of Psychology and Theology*, and *Pastoral Psychology*. It would be very strange indeed if such a rapidly developing field of knowledge were not to have important implications for the Church.

Third, Rollins and Kille point to 'changes in the field of biblical studies'. It is precisely to this area that the first part of our book has been devoted. It is these changes that have opened up the field of biblical studies to recognizing the importance of taking seriously the contextual or locational factors within the hermeneutical processes. In a sense, the contextual and locational factors of a sociological nature were recognized first, giving rise to approaches like liberation perspectives and feminist perspectives (see, for example, Slee, 2003, 2004). It would be very strange indeed if developments in biblical studies that took seriously such sociological perspectives were not to give equal recognition to psychological perspectives.

Fourth, Rollins and Kille argue that from these three changes eventually a fourth emerged which they characterize as a 'change in mutual perceptions between biblical scholars and psychologists'. The fourteen sections of Rollins and Kille's reader then proceed to illustrate the wide range of ways in which this interaction between psychology and biblical studies has proceeded. Against this background Rollins and Kille also re-emphasize the six specific research areas for psychological biblical criticism established during the early years of the Psychology and Biblical Studies programme unit of the Society of Biblical Literature when Rollins served as chair. These areas were described as: the history of research in biblical psychology; the development of a foundational psychological model capable of integrating different aspects of the research agenda; the role of psychological theory and research in biblical exegesis; the role of psychological theory and research in hermeneutics; the description and analysis of religious phenomena; and the examination of the impact of biblical texts on readers and communities, both pathogenic and therapeutic.

Our aim now in the rest of this book is to focus on just one of the interactions between psychology and biblical hermeneutics. This interaction concerns the contribution made by personality psychology. For us, this is the key interaction between the two disciplines of primary relevance to preachers. The insights of personality psychology are, in our view, central to biblical hermeneutics because we have come to appreciate how psychological type can help to shape the ways in which individuals read and proclaim the text of scripture. Moreover, if the model of personality we adopt is correct and there are indeed four different psychological functions which may shape our reading and proclamation of the text, then it follows that any one reading may be incomplete unless complemented by the other three. Such an understanding of psychological type gives new force to the Gospel injunctions to love the Lord your God 'with all your mind' or 'with all your soul' and not simply with your preferred psychological function. But this exhortation anticipates our later argument.

First, however, for this contribution from personality psychology to make sense, we need to examine carefully what we mean by personality and how this understanding of personality integrates within a wider theology of what it means to be human.

Christian doctrine

A primary task of the Christian theologian is to test the logic and internal coherence of claims made within Christian teaching. Our use of psychological insights into the interpretation and proclamation of scripture needs to be rigorously tested against (and integrated within) a coherent understanding of the major themes of Christian teaching as encapsulated, for example, by the key doctrines of creation, fall, salvation through the person of Christ, and sanctification through the work of the Holy Spirit.

The psychological insight on which we are drawing concerns the identification of the deep-seated components of human personality and belongs to the tradition known as the 'psychology of individual differences'. According to our understanding, the psychology of individual differences can be grounded within a 'theology of individual differences'. This notion of the theology of individual differences is first and foremost grounded in a Christian doctrine of creation. The biblical basis for this doctrine of creation is informed by Genesis 1.27:

> God created humankind in the image of God,
> in the image of God, God created them,
> male and female God created them.

The key insight provided by this biblical basis for a doctrine of creation is that God embraces diversity and that such diversity is reflected in those created in the image of God. The notion that God embraces diversity is clearly consistent with the Christian doctrine of Trinity and was also clearly anticipated within that strand in the opening books of the Old Testament which use a plural noun for God, as in Genesis 1.27.

In contrast with the narrative concerning Adam and Eve, a doctrine of creation grounded in Genesis 1.27 is committed theologically to recognizing both men and women to be created equally in the image of God, and to arguing that individual differences that are created equal (male and female) need to be accorded equal value and equal status. If such a theology of individual differences holds good for sex differences, then, by extension, such a theology should hold good also for other differences equally grounded in creation, that is to say in the intentionality of the divine creator. Such differences may well include those of ethnicity and those of personality. Before examining the implications of such a view, the Christian doctrine of creation needs to be set alongside the Christian doctrine of the fall.

The key point made by the Christian doctrine of the fall is that the image of the creator seen in the human creature is no longer unsullied. The image has been corrupted. The task to be undertaken by a sound theology of individual differences is to attempt to untangle those differences which can reasonably be posited to reflect the fall and those which persist as proper indicators of the image and of the intention of the divine creator. Those individual differences which reflect the corruption brought about by the fall must rightly be subject to the saving and trans-forming power of Christ (the doctrine of redemption) and the perfect-ing power of the Holy Spirit (the doctrine of sanctification). Those individual differences which reflect the divine image of the creator may need to be given proper respect and value in the hermeneutical dialogue between text and interpretation.

In the light of a doctrine of creation grounded in Genesis 1.27, the individual difference of sex (male and female) may be properly seen as reflecting creation rather than fall. As a consequence it becomes theo-logically inappropriate to call, say, on men to repent and to become women, or on women to repent and to become men. The argument seems equally strong to propose that the individual difference of ethnic-ity may be properly seen as reflecting creation rather than fall. Again, as a consequence, it becomes theologically inappropriate to call, say, on white people to repent and to become people of colour, or on people of colour to repent and to become white. There are, of course, enormous political implications that emerge from such a simple (and profound) theology of individual differences.

While the case may seem relatively clear-cut in respect of sex and ethnicity, the argument regarding individual differences in personality may prove to be somewhat more controversial. The problem arises, at least in part, from a real lack of clarity regarding ways in which the term 'personality' itself can be used, especially in colloquial usage. The professional debate needs to be sharpened, therefore, by distinguish-ing between two related, but potentially very distinct, terms ('person-ality' and 'character') and further by distinguishing between two related, but potentially very distinct, branches of psychology in which the term 'personality' is used (normal psychology and abnormal psychology).

Normal psychology is concerned with describing, understanding and interpreting variations within the normal population. In this context 'personality' is employed to define some of those normal variations. Abnormal psychology is concerned with describing, understanding and responding to psychological abnormalities and mental disorders of varying degrees of severity. In this context 'personality disorder' is employed to characterize dysfunctional behaviour. The ensuing discus-sion is rooted in the analysis of normal personality as distinct from a concern with personality disorders.

As generally employed within the normal psychology of individual differences, the term 'personality' is reserved for those deep-seated individual differences which reflect something of the individual's genetic roots, while character reflects individual qualities which are nearer the surface. Qualities which define personality are largely immutable (like sex and ethnicity), while qualities which define character are open to change and to development. Qualities which define personality should be morally neutral and value free (like sex and ethnicity), while qualities which define character should be highly significant in terms of morality and personal values.

An example of individual differences in personality is provided by the well-understood distinction between introversion and extraversion. Personality theory does not claim that extraverts are (in any sense) better or worse than introverts. Introverts and extraverts are just different and, as a consequence, introverts can do some things better than extraverts, and extraverts can do some things better than introverts. In other words, introverts do not need to become extraverts in order to become better people, nor do extraverts need to become introverts in order to become better people.

An example of individual differences in character is provided by the equally well-understood distinction between pride and humility. Moral theology is clear that one of these qualities is far superior to the other. Pride is looked upon as a consequence of the fall. This is not how in the beginning God intended people to be. Humility is looked upon as a sign of God's grace and redemption. This is how God intends redeemed people to become.

Thus, while normal personality is value neutral, character is heavily value laden. An extravert can develop a good character, sharing the fruits of the Spirit as described in Galatians 5 (love, joy, peace, patience, kindness, generosity, faithfulness, gentleness and self-control), or an extravert can develop a bad character, sharing the works of the flesh as also described in Galatians 5 (licentiousness, strife, jealousy, anger, quarrels, envy and drunkenness). An introvert also has equal opportunities to develop a good character or to develop a bad character.

Personality and character in the Bible

Another way of exploring the distinction between personality and character, in both a psychological and a theological sense, is to turn to the Gospels and to re-visit Jesus' profound insight into individual differences. This insight comes through perhaps most obviously in Luke's Gospel, but it is clearly there in the other Gospels as well.

In Luke 18, Jesus contrasts some basic individual differences observable in two visitors to the temple:

> Two men went up to the temple to pray, one a Pharisee and the other a tax collector. The Pharisee, standing by himself was praying thus, 'God, I thank you that I am not like other people, thieves, rogues, adulterers . . .' But the tax collector, standing far off, would not even look up to heaven.

Jesus' interest in this narrative is one based almost entirely on character, rather than on personality. The personality psychologist might well search for clues about the personality profile of the two men, but insufficient data are provided by Luke to enable much progress to be made. We could argue that an extravert might feel more comfortable standing up and praying out loud (the Pharisee), while an introvert might feel more comfortable standing far off (the tax collector), but this would be to miss the point of the story entirely. Jesus is not concerned so much with how these two characters say what they say, but with what they say. It is their words which give insight into their character.

The moral theologian, however, will find in this passage key insights about the attitude of mind and about the stuff of character which display being in the right relationship with God. Observation of the demeanour of the Pharisee and a close analysis of his language seems to lead to the clear diagnosis of an advanced state of pride. By contrast, however, observation of the demeanour of the tax collector and a close analysis of his language seems to lead to the clear recognition of natural humility. Jesus concludes this teaching with the telling evaluation that it was the tax collector who returned to his home justified (in the right relationship with God) rather than the Pharisee:

> For all who exalt themselves will be humbled, but all who humble themselves will be exalted.

In Luke 10, Jesus contrasts some basic individual differences observable in two sisters. Jesus entered a certain village where:

> Martha welcomed him into her home. She had a sister named Mary, who sat at the Lord's feet and listened to what he was saying. But Martha was distracted by her many tasks; so she came to him

and asked, 'Lord, do you not care that my sister has left me to do all the work by myself? Tell her then to help me.'

Jesus' interest in this narrative could be based on personality as well as character. Martha is portrayed as the extraverted sister. She is the one who welcomes visitors into the home. She is the one who is concerned with getting the social context right, having a feast and having contented guests. Mary is portrayed as the introverted sister. She is the one who feels at home sitting and listening, while others do the talking.

Clearly both sisters have important gifts to offer to Jesus out of the richness of their individual differences in personality. Jesus needs and welcomes the activity of the extravert. Jesus needs and welcomes the attention of the introvert. Both sisters, however, can be equally accused of showing flaws in their character. Mary becomes so wrapped up in her own introversion that she fails to notice and to respond to the growing tension in her sister. Martha becomes so wrapped up in her own extraversion that she fails to respect and to allow space for her sister's thirst for solitude and peace with Jesus. Just by the very nature of their differing personalities, introverts and extraverts often find it difficult to appreciate how things really look, how things really feel, from the other's perspective or from the other's point of view.

Both sisters show flaws in their character because of their failure to recognize and to respect individual differences. The extravert Martha just cannot understand why Mary does not see things her way and do things her way. The introvert Mary just cannot understand why Martha does not see things her way and do things her way. Personality psychology is needed to remind Martha that introverts are not failed extraverts, and to remind Mary that extraverts are not failed introverts.

In Luke 10 the conflict between extravert Martha and introvert Mary comes to a head when the extravert Martha speaks out her frustration and invites Jesus to take sides in the eternal battle between extraversion and introversion:

Lord, do you not care that my sister has left me to do all the work by myself? Tell her to help me.

Martha's outburst could be paraphrased thus:

Lord, do you not care that my sister sees things in a different way from me, and prefers to live life in a different way from me? Tell her it is wrong to be an introvert and that she needs to be more like me.

Jesus' response to Martha has been the subject of much debate among the commentators, and matters are not helped by some important disagreements among different ancient manuscripts regarding Jesus' actual words. Some commentators have seen Jesus' response as placing a higher value on the contemplative tradition (represented by Mary) than on the more active tradition (represented by Martha), but this is not the only interpretation. What is clear, however, is that Jesus refused to side with Martha and to tell Mary that she needed to change her personality.

In Luke 15 Jesus contrasts some basic individual differences observable in two brothers. Jesus said:

> There was a man who had two sons. The younger of them said to his father, 'Father, give me the share of the property that will belong to me.' So he divided his property between them.

Jesus' interest in this narrative could also be based on personality, as well as character. The way in which we read this narrative today, however, is likely to be highly coloured by the context in which we first encountered it. To some people this narrative is known as the Parable of the Prodigal Son. The very title focuses attention on the character flaws in the younger son. Here is the 'young waster' who needs to be taught a lesson or two in the school of life. Here is the 'young waster' who needs to repent and to reshape his character.

To some people the narrative is known as the Parable of the Lost Son. In Luke's compilation of material, the narrative stands in the third of a sequence, following the lost sheep and the lost coin. Now the very title refocuses attention on the concern of God to seek what is lost and to bring others into the kingdom.

The narrative might, however, be better styled as the Parable of the Two Sons. In this narrative Luke includes a great deal of detail about the personalities of the two sons, and on close examination they emerge as different as chalk and cheese. In fact their personality profiles are the very mirror image, one of the other. For example, the younger son, who ventures out to strange places and to meet strange people, displays all the outgoing characteristics of the extravert. The older son, on the other hand, who is content to stay in the relative isolation and solitude of the home farm, displays all the inward-looking characteristics of the introvert.

If this analysis holds good regarding the basic individual differences in the personality profiles of the two sons, two other aspects of the narrative become of central importance. The first observation is that both sons, not just the younger son, revealed fundamental flaws in their characters. Both were profoundly uncaring toward the father: the younger son when he left home and the older son when he refused to join the celebration. Both sons needed to hear the call to repentance and needed to change their character. The second observation is that the father loved and accepted both sons in spite of their flawed characters and in light of their individual differences in personality.

Conclusion

This chapter has demonstrated how psychological biblical criticism developed during the latter part of the twentieth century and has now become accepted as a distinctive section within the internationally respected Society of Biblical Literature. Our particular and distinctive contribution to psychological biblical criticism is rooted in an understanding of human personality and informed both by the psychology of individual differences and by the theology of individual differences. We have argued that the very idea of individual differences in personality is built into the Christian doctrine of creation and needs, therefore, to be taken seriously in the hermeneutical process. Our task now in the next chapter is to discover in greater detail how psychologists go about the discussion of personality.

Chapter 8

Models of Personality

Introduction

Personality psychology is a growing and complex field of study well discussed by a number of reviews and handbooks, including *The Personality Puzzle* by Funder (1997), *Handbook of Personality Psychology* by Hogan, Johnson and Briggs (1997), *Personality: Determinants, Dynamics and Potentials* by Caprara and Cervone (2000) and *Handbook of Research Methods in Personality Psychology* by Robins, Fraley and Krueger (2007). Our main purpose in this book is to work with and to develop implications from the model of personality known as psychological type theory. It would be misleading, however, to introduce psychological type theory without first discussing the broader family of personality theories to which this model belongs.

Alongside psychological type theory there are three other models of personality which have become generally well known within the psychology of religion and which have been shown to be useful for interpreting and understanding individual differences in areas of Christian living, Christian ministry and Christian mission. These are the three-dimensional model of personality proposed by Hans Eysenck and his associates (see Eysenck and Eysenck, 1985), the 'big five' factor model of personality proposed by Costa and McCrae (see Costa and McCrae, 1985), and the 'sixteen personality factor' model proposed by Raymond Cattell and his associates (see Cattell, Eber and Tatsuoka, 1970).

The aim of this chapter is to introduce the distinctive emphases of two of these different models of personality (those proposed by Eysenck and by Cattell) and to illustrate how they have been of service to the psychological study of religion and to the Christian community by examining the psychological profile of those called to ordained ministry.

The third model (proposed by Costa and McCrae) has been well discussed by Piedmont (1999) and by Saroglou (2002).

Personality in three dimensions

Eysenck's understanding of the structure of human personality is grounded on two fundamental assumptions, one concerning the nature of mental illness and the other concerning the independence of different dimensions of personality. Both assumptions are controversial. They have, nonetheless, led to the generation of significant insights into the nature of individual differences.

Eysenck's assumption concerning the nature of mental illness is this. He assumes a clear continuity between psychological health and psychological pathology. In other words, he envisages no categorical distinction between normal personality and abnormal personality. Rather, the psychologically ill display a particular concentration or intensity of characteristics that are present to greater or lesser degrees in the healthy population.

Looked at in another way, for Eysenck neurotic disorders are to be identified and located at one extreme of a dimension of normal personality. This dimension extends from emotional stability at the low-scoring end of the continuum, through emotional lability, to neurotic disorder at the opposite end of the same continuum.

Similarly, for Eysenck psychotic disorders are to be identified at one extreme of another dimension of normal personality. This dimension extends from tendermindedness at the low-scoring end of the continuum, through toughmindedness, to psychotic disorder at the opposite end of the same continuum.

Eysenck's assumption concerning the independence of different dimensions of personality demands that, for example, neuroticism and psychoticism are conceptualized as totally unrelated phenomena. When Eysenck set about developing instruments to measure these dimensions of personality, he determined that the questionnaire items which assessed each dimension should show no overlap with the other dimensions. The statistical tool employed to secure this independence is provided by factor analysis.

Alongside the two independent dimensions of personality defined at the extreme high-scoring end of the continua by neurotic disorders and by psychotic disorders, Eysenck's model included the third dimension of extraversion which is unrelated to psychopathology. This dimension extends from introversion at the low-scoring end of the continuum, through ambiversion, to extraversion at the opposite end of the same continuum.

The requirement that the three major dimensions of personality should be independent from one another (or, in mathematical terms, uncorrelated or orthogonal) means that knowing about someone's position on one of the dimensions cannot help predict that person's position on the other two dimensions. All three scores are therefore needed in order to locate an individual within Eysenck's three-dimensional personality space.

When Eysenck's scales are used to describe normal personality (as distinct from psychological pathology), the following three distinctions are made: between introversion and extraversion, between stability and neuroticism, and between tendermindedness and toughmindedness. 'Toughmindedness' is generally preferred to the term 'psychoticism', although the term 'neuroticism' is generally employed to describe individuals scoring in the normal range of high scores on that scale.

Individuals who record high scores within the normal range on all three scales could be described as toughminded neurotic extraverts. Individuals who record low scores on all three scales could be described as tenderminded stable introverts. All three scales, however, are designed to locate individuals on a continuum between low scores and high scores. There are no defined cutting-off points according to which, for example, introverts can be separated out from extraverts. Eysenck's model does not conceive of personality measurement as locating individuals in discrete categories so much as displaying how individual differences are graded on those three dimensions.

Defining the dimensions

In order to appreciate Eysenck's model of personality it is necessary to examine the definitions developed to establish what is being measured by the three scales. We turn attention, therefore, to the ways in which the constructs are defined in a recent edition of the test manual (Eysenck and Eysenck, 1991).

On the *extraversion scale,* the person who records high scores is described in the text as someone who is:

sociable, likes parties, has many friends, needs to have people to talk to, and does not like reading or studying by himself. He craves excitement, takes chances, often sticks his neck out, acts on the spur of the moment, and is generally an impulsive individual. He is fond of practical jokes, always has a ready answer, and generally likes change; he is carefree, easy-going, optimistic, and likes to 'laugh and be merry'. He prefers to keep moving and doing things. (p. 4)

By way of contrast, the introvert is described as someone who is:

a quiet, retiring sort of person, introspective, fond of books rather than people; he is reserved and distant except to intimate friends. He tends to plan ahead, 'looks before he leaps', and distrusts the impulse of the moment. He does not like excitement, takes matters of everyday life with proper seriousness, and likes a well-ordered mode of life. (p. 4)

On the *neuroticism scale*, the person who records high scores is described as:

an anxious, worrying individual, moody and frequently depressed. He is likely to sleep badly, and to suffer from various psycho-somatic disorders. He is overly emotional, reacting too strongly to all sorts of stimuli, and finds it difficult to get back on an even keel after each emotionally arousing experience. His strong emotional reactions interfere with his proper adjustment, making him react in irrational, sometimes rigid ways. (p. 4)

By way of contrast, the person who records low scores on the neuroticism scale is described as someone who:

tends to respond emotionally only slowly and generally weakly, and to return to baseline quickly after emotional arousal; he is usually calm, even-tempered, controlled and unworried. (p. 5)

On the *psychoticism scale*, the person who records high scores is described as someone who:

may be cruel and inhumane, lacking in feeling and empathy, and altogether insensitive. He is hostile to others, even his own kith and kin, and aggressive, even to loved ones. He has a liking for odd and unusual things, and a disregard for danger; he likes to make fools of other people, and to upset them. Socialisation is a concept which is relatively alien to high P scorers; empathy, feelings of guilt, and sensitivity to other people are notions which are strange and unfamiliar to them. (p. 6)

By way of contrast, the person who records low scores on the psychoticism scale is described as someone who is empathic, unselfish, altruistic, warm, peaceful, and generally more pleasant, although possibly less socially decisive.

Clergy and the three dimensions of personality

A key question which has fascinated psychologists over the years is whether people with some specific personality profiles are more likely than others to be drawn into the clerical profession (Dittes, 1971). Until recently, however, relatively little systematic research has addressed this issue. In a foundational study, building on pioneering work by Towler and Coxon (1979), Francis (1991) administered the Eysenck Personality Questionnaire to 155 male and 97 female Anglican ordinands. The findings were quite surprising.

The male ordinands emerged as significantly more introverted than men in general. In fact their extraversion scores were closer to the population norms for women than for men. This finding led to the conclusion that male clergy may tend to project a feminine personality profile, at least in the Anglican Church. Certainly this would fit with the view that the Anglican Church has become a highly feminized environment, now much more readily accessible by women than by men.

The female ordinands, on the other hand, emerged as significantly more extraverted than women in general. In fact their extraversion scores were closer to the population norms for men than for women. Moreover, the female ordinands were also more stable than women in general and more toughminded than women in general. In fact their neuroticism and psychoticism scores were closer to the population norms for men than for women. This finding led to the conclusion that female clergy may, at that time at least, tend to project a masculine personality profile. Certainly this would fit with the way in which in the late 1980s clergywomen were still having to adopt the pioneering stance of fighting for admission to the priesthood, which was not to come in the Church of England until 1994.

More recent studies among Anglican clergy have shown less pronounced differences between the clergymen and the clergywomen (Robbins, Francis and Rutledge, 1997).

Studies among other denominations have built on these studies among Anglican clergy. Louden and Francis (1999) reported on a sample of 1,168 Roman Catholic parochial secular priests. In terms of the two major dimensions of extraversion and neuroticism these priests displayed a personality profile more characteristic of women. In other words, Roman Catholic priests were more introverted than men in general and more neurotic than men in general. In terms of the third major dimension of psychoticism, the Roman Catholic priests displayed a clearly masculine profile.

Robbins, Francis, Haley and Kay (2001) reported on a sample of 1,102 male Methodist ministers and 237 female Methodist ministers. Their findings, too, supported the view that ministry may appeal particularly to men who value and display the tenderminded characteristics associated with femininity and to women who value and display the stable personality characteristics associated with masculinity.

The tendency for male clergy to display significantly lower extraversion scores does not extend to all denominations. The two studies reported by Francis and Kay (1995) among Pentecostal ministry candidates and by Kay (2000) among Pentecostal ministers suggest that male Pentecostal clergy are at least as extraverted as men in general and possibly more so. Then the study by Francis and Robbins (2004) found that pastors associated with the New Churches are even more extraverted than those associated with the classic Pentecostal Churches.

Personality in sixteen factors

In some ways Hans Eysenck's approach and Raymond Cattell's approach to personality assessment have much in common. Both were committed to exploring the structure of individual differences through empirical observation and through mathematical analyses. In other ways their approaches are radically different. Eysenck concentrated on higher-order personality dimensions, while Cattell concentrated on lower-order personality traits. As a consequence, Eysenck's instruments are able to report on only three dimensions, while Cattell's instruments are generally able to report on sixteen traits. Cattell, some would argue, is, as a consequence, able to provide a much richer description of personality. Others maintain that Cattell's model provides unnecessary information overload.

Eysenck assumed that the major dimensions of personality were orthogonal and uncorrelated. His mathematical models forced clarity between the dimensions by rejecting personality indicators or questionnaire items which did not meet this criterion. Cattell expected his lower-order personality traits to reflect interaction one with another. Cattell, some would argue, is simply being true to the way things are. Others maintain that Cattell is not thinking clearly enough about the differences between his hypothesized traits.

Eysenck assumed that good personality measures needed to demonstrate a high level of internal consistency reliability (which would be reflected in high alpha coefficients). In other words, all the items in one of Eysenck's scales were designed to assess the same tightly defined domain. Cattell expected his scales to measure more broadly based constructs and so he resisted the pressures for high levels of internal homogeneity. He would see a high alpha coefficient as an indicator of a poor scale since the domain would be too tightly defined. Cattell, some would argue, has therefore developed more interesting personality constructs. Others maintain that Cattell is simply creating poor measuring instruments.

Defining the factors

In order to appreciate Cattell's model of personality, it is necessary to examine each of the sixteen personality factors in turn, as proposed by the Sixteen Personality Factor Questionnaire (16PFQ: Cattell, Eber and Tatsuoka, 1970). This instrument was designed for use among adults. The factors are known by a letter or by a letter and number. Not all the letters of the alphabet are used (there is no factor D, J, K or P), so do not be taken by surprise when some letters do not appear. The factors are then best identified by reference to the simple word descriptions of the low scoring and high scoring ends of the scale. Conventionally some brief description is then given of the high scorers and of the low scorers.

Factor A assesses a trait from *reserved* to *outgoing*. It examines how ready people are to be warmly involved with others. High scorers on this factor are energized by their warm involvement with other people, caring for them and being concerned with their welfare. Low scorers use less energy associating with people and therefore have more energy for pursuits which do not involve interaction with others.

Factor B assesses a trait from *less intelligent* to *more intelligent*. It examines how able people are intellectually. High scorers on this factor tend to be quick to grasp ideas, and are usually fast learners. Low scorers tend to be slow to learn and to grasp new ideas. They tend to formulate concrete and literal interpretations of evidence.

Factor C assesses a trait from *emotionally less stable* to *emotionally stable*. It examines how much people feel in control of the daily demands of life. High scorers on this factor generally feel in control of life and its demands. They adjust well to changing circumstances and do not feel bowed down by the pressures of living. Low scorers are likely to become dissatisfied with life, feeling unable to cope with its pressures and changes. They tend to lurch from one challenge to another.

Factor E assesses a trait from *deferential* to *dominant*. It examines how much people exert influence over others. High scorers on this factor express their views and opinions strongly. They may enjoy positions of power and leadership in which they find themselves controlling other people. Low scorers tend to be much more influenced in their decision-making by the views and beliefs of others. They tend to be self-effacing, wishing to avoid conflict by deferring to the views of others.

Factor F assesses a trait from *serious* to *lively*. It examines how much people prefer excitement-seeking as opposed to seriousness. High scorers on this factor express themselves spontaneously. They enjoy stimulating social situations and the excitement of being at the centre of the stage. Low scorers have a serious, pessimistic attitude to life. They consider the implications of things carefully before speaking or acting.

Factor G assesses a trait from *expedient* to *rule-conscious*. It examines how much people are concerned to keep the rules and regulations of their society. High scorers on this factor regard themselves as principled people. They tend to be law-abiding, self-controlled, conscientious citizens whose behaviour is guided by rules and regulations. Low scorers tend to be expedient and possibly rebellious. They are not socially conforming, and believe that people have the right to make their own moral and ethical choices.

Factor H assesses a trait from *shy* to *socially bold*. It examines how much people feel at ease in social surroundings. High scorers on this factor are responsive, genial people who relish being at the centre of social situations. They are among the first to initiate social contacts between others at a party and are not shy to make the first move. Low scorers are socially timid people who dislike mingling with others. They tend to avoid social groups, and prefer to stay in the background.

Factor I assesses a trait from *toughminded* to *sensitive*. It examines how much people prefer to make decisions on the basis of subjective feelings rather than hard data. High scorers on this factor are concerned primarily with values and emotional feelings when they are making decisions, particularly decisions which will impinge on the lives of others. Low scorers are concerned primarily with objectivity. When making decisions they rely on logical analysis of the matter in hand, rather than the consequences for other people's feelings.

Factor L assesses a trait from *trusting* to *vigilant*. It examines how much people question the motives behind what others say and do. High scorers on this factor are vigilant about others' intentions, questioning their motives and suspecting that things are not as they might appear. They are concerned about what others are saying behind their backs. Low scorers tend to assume that others are what they seem to be and they trust the motives of others.

Factor M assesses a trait from *practical* to *abstracted*. It examines how much people allow their attention to wander beyond the immediate situation to abstract ideas. High scorers on this factor spend much time in theoretical consideration and generation of ideas. They speculate on a variety of approaches to problems. Low scorers focus their attention on the external environment of the five senses. They are keen on working out the practicalities of a project, planning its detail and gathering the necessary facts and materials.

Factor N assesses a trait from *forthright* to *private*. It examines how much people open up to others in terms of disclosing private information about themselves. High scorers on this factor do not open up readily to others. They are personally guarded, valuing their privacy and keeping their problems to themselves. Low scorers display an open, unguarded style toward other people. They are spontaneous with others, talking about all aspects of their background, feelings, hopes and fears.

Factor O assesses a trait from *self-assured* to *apprehensive*. It examines how much people worry about things, before and after the event, and how much they feel apprehensive and insecure. High scorers on this factor worry about what they say and do and about whether they come up to other people's expectations. They feel very downhearted and hurt when people criticize them. Low scorers feel confident and cheerful about themselves, not worrying what other people think of them. They do not feel guilty about their actions and mistakes.

Factor Q1 assesses a trait from *conservative* to *open to change*. It examines how much people are open to change and to experimentation. High scorers on this factor are continually open to new ideas and experiences. They tend to be bored by routine and repetitive tasks, preferring to pioneer new ways of doing things. Low scorers value the tradition of the past, feeling secure when they stay with familiar, well-tried methods. They are happy with routine.

Factor Q2 assesses a trait from *group-dependent* to *self-reliant*. It examines how much people prefer to do things alone, as opposed to doing things with others. High scorers on this factor prefer to do things alone. They make decisions based on their own thinking and judgements. Low scorers desire to belong to a group and to be part of a group identity. They value the input of others in making their decisions or choices.

Factor Q3 assesses a trait from *tolerant of disorder* to *perfectionist*. It examines how much people plan ahead in an organized fashion because they want things done correctly. High scorers on this factor are perfectionists. They have definite personal standards to which they adhere and they are reluctant to cut corners so that tasks can be finished more quickly. Low scorers are adaptable, flexible and spontaneous. They tend to react to circumstances as they happen and are willing to suspend one activity for another.

Factor Q4 assesses a trait from *relaxed* to *tense*. It examines how much people feel physically tense and irritable. High scorers on this factor experience frequent rises in their levels of physical tension, muscle tension and emotional fatigue. They tend to feel annoyed easily by comparatively trivial incidents. Low scorers tend to feel calm and tranquil. Others' actions do not make them irritable or impatient.

Clergy and the sixteen personality factors

Using a recent edition of Cattell's instrument, the 16PF5 (Cattell, Cattell and Cattell, 1993), David Musson reported a survey of 332 male and 250 female Anglican stipendiary clergy in the Church of England (Musson, 2001, 2002). In reporting his findings Musson decided not to use factor B, the measure of intelligence. Among the other fifteen factors, Musson found that male Anglican clergy differed from the population norms for British men in general in all but three factors. No differences were found between male clergy and men in general in terms of factor C (a trait from emotionally less stable to emotionally stable), factor H (a trait from shy to socially bold), and factor Q2 (a trait from group-dependent to self-reliant).

Male clergy scored significantly higher on factor A, indicating that they were more outgoing and less reserved than men in general. This is consistent with the view that clergy need to be people-centred in a pastoral ministry that endeavours to stand alongside others in their need as well as actively recruit new adherents through warm, personal contact.

Male clergy scored significantly lower on factor E, indicating that they were more deferential and less dominant than men in general. This is consistent with the fact that, in working with volunteers, clergy need to be accommodating to other people's perspectives and appreciative of efforts made in the service of the Church.

Male clergy scored significantly lower on factor F, indicating that they were more serious and less lively than men in general. This is consistent with the idea that clergy display a serious, cautious attitude to life, thinking carefully before they speak and generally holding back from spontaneity.

Male clergy scored significantly higher on factor G, indicating that they were more rule-conscious and less expedient than men in general. This is consistent with the idea that clergy are themselves both under authority and the guardians of moral behaviour.

Male clergy scored particularly high on factor I, indicating that they were much more sensitive and much less toughminded than men in general. This is consistent with emotional sensitivity being core to such roles as counselling and pastoral visiting.

Male clergy scored particularly low on factor L, indicating that they were much more trusting and much less vigilant than men in general. This is consistent with the view that clergy see goodness and sincerity in others and generally perceive people as trustworthy.

Male clergy scored significantly higher on factor M, indicating that they were more abstracted and less practical than men in general. This is consistent with the view that clergy focus on what is beyond the present, and are more concerned with ideas and concepts than with practical details.

Male clergy scored significantly lower on factor N, indicating that they were more forthright and less private than men in general. This is consistent with the view that clergy are comfortable disclosing personal information about their lives and faith-journeys rather than maintaining personal privacy.

Male clergy scored significantly higher on factor O, indicating that they were more apprehensive and less self-assured than men in general. This is consistent with the view that clergy experience low levels of self-confidence and are keen to gain the approval of parishioners.

Male clergy scored significantly higher on factor Q1, indicating that they were more open to change and less conservative than men in general. This is consistent with the view that clergy are receptive to new ideas and willing to change their methods to improve their ministries.

Male clergy scored significantly lower on factor Q3, indicating that they were more tolerant of disorder and less perfectionist than men in general. This is consistent with the view that clergy often need to be reactive to situations that arise in ministry, having to handle unexpected needs and demands from their parishioners.

Male clergy scored significantly lower on factor Q4, indicating that they were more relaxed and less tense than men in general. This is consistent with the view that clergy need to handle complex human situations and emotions without letting them have negative implications for their own health and well-being.

Musson's subsequent comparison of the profiles of male and female clergy confirmed the findings of studies using other measures that some of the expected gender differences between men and women are actually reversed among the clergy. Contrary to the usual sex differences in personality profile found in the general population, female clergy were shown to be less outgoing (factor A), more emotionally stable (factor C), more dominant (factor E), less rule-conscious (factor G), less emotionally sensitive (factor I), less apprehensive (factor O), and more open to change (Q1) than male clergy.

Conclusion

Discussions of the two very different models of personality proposed by Hans Eysenck and by Raymond Cattell have illustrated the rich diversity which exists among personality psychologists and how different models of personality can be employed to illuminate an area of practical relevance to Christian ministry. These models are unlikely, however, to appear particularly fruitful for illuminating the questions raised by the examination of hermeneutics within the first part of this book. This is the case for two different reasons.

The first reason is this. Working as psychologists concerned to describe the human situation as they experienced it (in a fallen world), both Eysenck and Cattell take a very broad view of the notion of 'personality'. Their use of the term is much broader than the narrower definition advanced above in Chapter 7, where we wanted to distinguish between, on the one hand, those fundamental individual differences (like sex and ethnicity) which reflect the intentionality and the image of the divine creator, and on the other hand those individual differences which reflect the consequences of the fall, like psychopathology and the corruption of character. The next chapter, therefore, turns attention to the model of personality that is concerned with a small number of individual differences clearly distinct from either issues of psychopathology or issues of character.

The second reason is this. The two models of personality proposed by Eysenck and Cattell have failed to deal with those psychological functions which the first part of this book have identified as key to hermeneutics, namely the two processes of perception and of evaluation. The next chapter, therefore, turns to the model of personality that gives due attention to these two processes.

Chapter 9

Understanding Psychological Type

Introduction

The Jungian model of psychological type offers a very different understanding of personality and individual differences from the models
developed by Hans Eysenck and by Raymond Cattell as discussed in the
previous chapter. It is the Jungian model of psychological type that is
fundamental to the psychological science of hermeneutics.

The aims of the present chapter are to begin by discussing the significant ways in which psychological type theory differs from the models of
personality outlined in the previous chapter and then to define with care
the four key constructs on which psychological type theory is built: the
two orientations (extraversion and introversion), the two perceiving
processes (sensing and intuition), the two judging processes (feeling and
thinking), and the two attitudes toward the outer world (judging and
perceiving). Finally, the chapter examines ways in which psychological
type can be measured or assessed.

Psychological type theory

The idea of psychological type was first proposed by Carl Jung and
described in his book, *Psychological Types* (Jung, 1971). There are four
main components to this theory. The theory begins by proposing the
notion of the two *orientations* defined as *introversion* (I) and extraversion (E). The orientations are concerned with the source of psychological energy. According to the theory, the introvert looks inwards for
psychological energy, while the extravert looks outwards for psychological energy.

The second and third components of the theory are concerned with the two main psychological processes. One psychological process concerns the ways in which we gather information. This is the *perceiving* process or the process concerned with perception. In terms of the perceiving process, some people prefer *sensing* (S), while others prefer *intuition* (N). According to the theory, these two types look at the world in very different ways.

The other psychological process concerns the ways in which we make decisions. This is the *judging* process or the process concerned with evaluation. In terms of the judging process, some people prefer *thinking* (T), while others prefer *feeling* (F). According to the theory, these two types come to decisions about the world in very different ways.

The fourth component suggests that we prefer to use one of these processes in the outer world and the other process in the inner world. In other words, some people prefer to use judging in the outer world and to use perceiving in the inner world, while other people prefer to use judging in the inner world and to use perceiving in the outer world. Many of those who have built on Jung's theory of psychological type have proposed, therefore, a fourth indicator, often characterized as *attitude toward the outer world*. In terms of attitude toward the outer world, some people prefer to use *judging* (J) and others prefer to use *perceiving* (P). These two types present very different images to the outer world.

At this point it is important to draw attention to the very distinctive ways in which Jung uses the words 'judging' and 'perceiving'. Both words need to be used in the technical ways they have been defined above. 'Judging' has nothing to do with being judgemental. 'Perceiving' has nothing to do with being perceptive.

There are two key characteristics which make psychological type theory very different from the two models of personality proposed by Hans Eysenck and by Raymond Cattell. These two characteristics are concerned with the idea of type categories and with the idea of psychological health.

The first important characteristic of type theory concerns the distinction between psychological type categories and personality dimensions or continua. For example, Eysenck characterizes introversion and extraversion as two ends of a single continuum. Eysenck's extraversion scale functions like a metre ruler or a thermometer. Individuals can be placed anywhere on that continuum. On that continuum, there is no central cut-off point which can distinguish whether you fit as an introvert or as an extravert. Individuals are simply compared one with another as scoring higher or lower on this continuum.

Jung's notion of introversion and extraversion, however, is one of two distinct types. According to Jung's theory, it is possible to categorize an individual either as an introvert or as an extravert. Ease of classification depends on levels of self-awareness and clarity of preference.

One way of looking at Jung's model of psychological type is by comparing it with our experience of handedness. We are all generally equipped with two hands, but we instinctively prefer one over the other. Consequently we develop more skills with our preferred hand, and, at the same time, neglect to develop the less preferred hand to its full potential. If we were to try to take notes, say in a lecture or in a sermon, with our less preferred hand, we would notice three things. It would take a lot more concentration and make it less easy for us to listen to what is being said. It would be slower to write and much less easy to read. It would be much more tiring and draining on our energy resources.

Just as we all generally benefit from a right hand and a left hand, Jung suggests that we are all equipped with the ability to use extraversion and to use introversion, but we instinctively prefer one over the other. Consequently we develop more skills with our preferred orientation (either extraversion or introversion) and at the same time neglect to develop the less preferred orientation to its full potential.

There are lots of reasons why some people operate outside their preferred mode for much of their life. There was a time when children were all encouraged (or forced) at school to write with the right hand, irrespective of their instinctive preference. For some, this seems to lead to illegible handwriting, and for others to more serious malfunctioning. There are lots of reasons, too, why some people as they are growing up are encouraged (or forced) to operate outside their preferred orientation.

Sometimes as soon as young introverts are taken to the nursery school they begin to learn that it is wise to speak out and to pretend to be an extravert in order to get noticed. Some primary schools prefer extraverted behaviour and encourage it.

Sometimes if young extraverts are growing up in a predominantly introverted household, they begin to learn that it is wise to keep quiet and to pretend to be an introvert in order to keep out of sight and out of trouble. Some homes prefer introverted behaviour and encourage it.

In such cases it may not be until considerably later in life that suppressed introverts or suppressed extraverts discover who they really are and claim their true psychological preference. The problem about living out-of-type is that it can be an inefficient use of energy resources and sometimes it can be quite debilitating. In some of his writings Jung speaks about the *persona* or the mask which people choose to wear (or which they put on unknowingly) and behind which the real self withers. The joy about studying psychological type theory is that it sometimes helps us to see more clearly who we really are and to claim our true identity.

The second important characteristic of type theory concerns the distinction between healthy personality and unhealthy personality. For example, Eysenck builds his model of personality around key concepts of psychological pathology, namely neuroticism and psychoticism. Very high scorers on Eysenck's neuroticism scale or on Eysenck's psychoticism scale may well begin to wonder about their psychological health and about their normal levels of psychological functioning.

Jung's notion of psychological type, however, is totally benign. Neither the language nor the concepts of psychological type theory have anything to do with psychological pathology. Learning about your psychological type is a completely non-threatening experience. There is nothing to fear from completing a psychological test concerned with type theory.

Having given a very brief introduction to the two orientations (introversion and extraversion), the two perceiving processes (sensing and intuition), the two judging processes (thinking and feeling) and the two attitudes to the outer world (judging and perceiving), we will introduce each in greater depth. Our recommendation is that our readers might like to make their own personality assessment while reading these descriptions. Such assessment will come in useful when applying the theory to hermeneutics in the closing chapters of this book.

Introversion and extraversion

Introversion and extraversion describe the two preferred orientations of the inner world and the outer world. Introverts prefer to focus their attention on the inner world of ideas and draw their energy from that inner world. When introverts are tired and need energizing they look to the inner world. Extraverts prefer to focus their attention on the outer world of people and things and draw their energy from that outer world. When extraverts are tired and need energizing they look to the outer world. This chapter presents the introvert perspective first, followed by the extravert perspective.

Introverts like quiet for concentration. They want to be able to shut off the distractions of the outer world and turn inwards. They often experience trouble in remembering names and faces. They can work at one solitary project for a long time without interruption. When they are engaged in a task in the outer world they may become absorbed in the ideas behind that task.

Introverts work best alone and may resent distractions and interruptions from other people. They dislike being interrupted by the telephone, tend to think things through before acting, and may spend so long in thought that they miss the opportunity to act.

Introverts prefer to learn by reading rather than by talking with others. They may also prefer to communicate with others in writing, rather than face-to-face or over the phone; this is particularly the case if they have something unpleasant to communicate.

Introverts are oriented to the inner world. They focus on ideas, concepts and inner understanding. They are reflective, may consider deeply before acting, and they probe inwardly for stimulation.

Extraverts like variety and action. They want to be able to shut off the distractions of the inner world and turn outward. They are good at remembering faces and names and enjoy meeting people and introducing people. They can become impatient with long, slow jobs. When they are working in the company of other people they may become more interested in how others are doing the job than in the job itself.

Extraverts like to have other people around them in the working environment, and enjoy the stimulus of sudden interruptions and telephone calls. Extraverts like to act quickly and decisively, even when it is not totally appropriate to do so.

Extraverts prefer to learn a task by talking it through with other people. They prefer to communicate with other people face-to-face or over the phone, rather than in writing. They often find that their own ideas become clarified through communicating them to others. Extraverts are oriented to the outer world. They focus on people and things. They prefer to learn by trial and error and they do so with confidence. They are active people, and they scan the outer environment for stimulation.

If, having read these contrasting descriptions, you are still puzzled about your real preference between introversion and extraversion, a very good test is to examine what makes you tired and then how you react when you are feeling tired.

For introverts it is the outer world of people which makes them really tired and which can do so quite quickly. When introverts spend a full day working with people and talking with others, they will go home worn out, exhausted and puzzled as to how extraverts keep going in the company of others. In fact, at the end of such a day extraverts seem even more full of life than when the day started.

At the end of a tiring day there is nothing introverts want to do more than to go home, close the door, and be on their own. They re-energize and re-charge their batteries by being on their own.

For extraverts it is the inner world of ideas and thoughts which makes them really tired and which can do so quite quickly. When extraverts spend a full day working with books and writing alone, they will go home worn out, exhausted and puzzled as to how introverts keep going in their own company. In fact, at the end of such a day introverts seem even more full of life than when the day started.

At the end of a tiring day there is nothing extraverts want to do more than to go out and to enjoy the company of others. They re-energize and re-charge their batteries by being with other people.

Given such a fundamental difference between introverts and extraverts, it is not surprising that they can sometimes easily misunderstand each other. On the one hand, extraverts may experience introverts as people who are withdrawn, aloof and very difficult to get to know. On the other hand, introverts may experience extraverts as people who are shallow and lacking in any real depth. The truth of the matter is that introverts and extraverts present themselves to the world in very different ways.

Sensing and intuition

Sensing and intuition describe the two preferences associated with the *perceiving process*. They describe different preferences used to acquire information. Sensing types focus on the realities of a situation as perceived by the senses. Intuitive types focus on the possibilities, meanings and relationships, the 'big picture' that goes beyond sensory information. This chapter presents the intuitive perspective first, followed by the sensing perspective.

Individuals who prefer *intuition* develop insight into complexity. They have the ability to see abstract, symbolic and theoretical relationships, and the capacity to see future possibilities. They put their reliance on inspiration rather than on past experience. Their interest is in the new and untried. They trust their intuitive grasp of meanings and relationships.

Individuals with a preference for intuition are aware of new challenges and possibilities. They see quickly beyond the information they have been given or the materials they have to hand to the possibilities and challenges which these offer. They are often discontented with the way things are and wish to improve them. They become bored quickly and dislike doing the same thing repeatedly.

Intuitive types enjoy learning new skills. They work in bursts of energy, powered by enthusiasm, and then enjoy slack periods between activities. Intuitive types follow their inspirations and hunches. They may reach conclusions too quickly and misconstrue the information or get the facts wrong. They dislike taking too much time to secure precision.

Intuitive types may tend to imagine that things are more complex than they really are: they tend to over-complexify things. They are curious about why things are the way they are and may prefer to raise questions rather than to find answers.

Intuitive types perceive with memory and associations. They see patterns and meanings and assess possibilities. They are good at reading between the lines and projecting possibilities for the future. They prefer to go always for the big picture. They prefer to let the mind inform the eyes.

Individuals who prefer *sensing* develop keen awareness of present experience. They have acute powers of observation, good memory for facts and details, the capacity for realism, and the ability to see the world as it is. They rely on experience rather than theory. They put their trust in what is known and in the conventional.

Individuals with a preference for sensing are aware of the uniqueness of each individual event. They develop good techniques of observation and they recognize the practical way in which things work now.

Sensing types like to develop an established way of doing things and gain enjoyment from exercising skills which they have already learnt. Repetitive work does not bore them. They are able to work steadily with a realistic idea of how long a task will take.

Sensing types usually reach their conclusion step by step, observing each piece of information carefully. They are not easily inspired to interpret the information in front of them and they may not trust inspiration when it comes. They are very careful about getting the facts right and are good at engaging with detail.

Sensing types may fail to recognize complexity in some situations, and consequently over-simplify tasks. They are good at accepting the current reality as the given situation in which to work. They would much rather work with the present information than speculate about future possibilities.

Sensing types perceive clearly with the five senses. They attend to practical and factual details, and they are in touch with physical realities. They attend to the present moment and prefer to confine their attention to what is said and done. They observe the small details of everyday life and attend to step-by-step experience. They prefer to let the eyes tell the mind.

If, having read these contrasting descriptions, you are still puzzled about your real preference between sensing and intuition, a very good test is to examine how you react when you are feeling tired. It is your less preferred function which is most likely to let you down.

For intuitive types it is the less preferred function of sensing which lets them down when they are tired. When tired, intuitive types fail to notice things, begin to lose things, and get basic facts wrong. A good example is when the intuitive type drives to a meeting in an unfamiliar town, parks the car in a side street while thinking about the meeting, gets out of the car and completely fails to pick up any clues about the location. Cars parked in this way can be very hard to find after the meeting.

For sensing types it is the less preferred function of intuition which lets them down when they are tired. When tired, sensing types fail to see how the pieces fit together, cannot work out what things really mean, and begin to sink under piles of undigested information. A good example is how the sensing type may puzzle for hours over an apparently intractable problem and just cannot get a new angle on it, or see it from a new perspective. Problems tackled in this way can be very hard to resolve.

Given such a fundamental difference between sensing and intuitive types, it is not surprising that they can sometimes easily misunderstand each other. On the one hand, sensing types may experience intuitive types as people who are impractical daydreamers and impossible to pin down to face facts and reality. On the other hand, intuitive types may experience sensing types as people who are far too literalistic, materialistic, unimaginative and dull. The truth of the matter is that sensing and intuitive types perceive the world in very different ways.

Thinking and feeling

Thinking and feeling describe the two preferences associated with the *judging process*. They describe different preferences by which decisions are reached. Individuals who prefer thinking make decisions based on objective, logical analysis. Individuals who prefer feeling make decisions by subjective values based on how people will be affected. This chapter presents the thinking perspective first, followed by the feeling perspective.

Individuals who prefer *thinking* develop clear powers of logical analysis. They develop the ability to weigh facts objectively and to predict consequences, both intended and unintended. They develop a stance of impartiality. They are characterized by a sense of fairness and justice.

Individuals with a preference for thinking are good at putting things in logical order. They are able to put people in their place when they consider it necessary. They are able to take tough decisions and to reprimand others. They are also able to be firm and toughminded about themselves.

Thinking types need to be treated fairly and to see that other people are treated fairly as well. They are inclined to respond more to other people's ideas than to other people's feelings. They may inadvertently hurt other people's feelings without recognizing that they are doing so.

Thinking types are able to anticipate and predict the logical outcomes of other people's choices. They can see the humour rather than the human pain in bad choices and wrong decisions taken by others. Thinking types prefer to look at life from the outside as a spectator.

Thinking types are able to develop good powers of critical analysis. They use objective and impersonal criteria in reaching decisions. They follow logically the relationships between cause and effect. They develop characteristics of being firm-minded and prizing logical order. They may appear sceptical.

Individuals who prefer *feeling* develop a personal emphasis on values and standards. They appreciate what matters most to themselves and what matters most to other people. They develop an understanding of people, a wish to affiliate with people and a desire for harmony. They are characterized by their capacity for warmth, and by qualities of empathy and compassion.

Individuals with a preference for feeling like harmony and will work hard to bring about harmony between other people. They dislike telling other people unpleasant things or reprimanding other people. They take into account other people's feelings. Feeling types need to have their own feelings recognized as well. They need praise and affirmation. They are good at seeing the personal effects of choices on their own lives and on other people's lives as well.

Feeling types are sympathetic individuals. They take a great interest in the people behind the job and respond to other people's values as much as to their ideas. They enjoy pleasing people. Feeling types look at life from the inside. They live life as committed participants and find it less easy to stand back and to form an objective view of what is taking place.

Feeling types develop good skills at applying personal priorities. They are good at weighing human values and motives, both their own and other people's. They are characterized by qualities of empathy and sympathy. They prize harmony and trust.

If, having read these contrasting descriptions, you are still puzzled about your real preference between thinking and feeling, a very good test is to examine how you react when you are feeling tired. It is your less preferred function which is most likely to let you down.

For thinking types it is the less preferred function of feeling which lets them down when they are tired. When tired, thinking types fail to take into account other people's feelings, fail to predict other people's emotional reactions, and can really hurt other people without intending to do so. A good example is how thinking types may analyse out the issues behind a conflict and then expect the people involved in the conflict to agree with and be helped by the analysis. The analysis may well be true and fair, but nonetheless deeply hurtful and capable of provoking anger.

For feeling types it is the less preferred function of thinking which lets them down when they are tired. When tired, feeling types fail to be able to analyse out what is actually going on in a situation. They get drawn into the situation, and they find it very difficult to stand back and to be objective. They can themselves become quite easily hurt. A good example is how feeling types may try all too hard to empathize with both sides of a quarrel, or with both parties in a conflict. Feeling types may long so much to bring comfort to those who are distressed and to introduce harmony to where there is conflict that they end up being torn apart themselves by the situation they want to resolve.

Given such a fundamental difference between thinking and feeling types, it is not surprising that they can sometimes and so easily misunderstand each other. On the one hand, feeling types may experience thinking types as people who are cold and sometimes even irritatingly condescending. On the other hand, thinking types may experience feeling types as people who are overly emotional and sometimes even sentimental and irrational. The truth of the matter is that feeling and thinking types deal with the world in very different ways.

Judging and perceiving

Judging and perceiving describe the two preferred attitudes toward the outer world. Individuals who prefer to relate to the outer world with a judging process present a planned and orderly approach to life. They prefer to have a settled system in place and display a preference for closure. Individuals who prefer to relate to the outer world with a perceiving process present a flexible and spontaneous approach to life. They prefer to keep plans and organizations to a minimum and display a preference for openness. This chapter presents the judging perspective first, followed by the perceiving perspective.

Judging types schedule projects so that each step gets done on time. They like to get things finished and settled, and to know that the finished product is in place. They work best when they can plan their work in advance and follow that plan. Judging types use lists and agendas to structure their day and to plan their actions. They may dislike interruption from the plans they have made and are reluctant to leave the task in hand even when something more urgent arises.

Judging types tend to be satisfied once they reach a judgement or have made a decision, both about people and things. They dislike having to revise their decision and take fresh information into account. They like to get on with a task as soon as possible once the essential things are at hand. As a consequence, judging types may decide to act too quickly.

When individuals take a judging attitude toward the outer world, they are using the preferred *judging process*, thinking or feeling, outwardly. Their attitude to life is characterized by deciding and planning, organizing and scheduling, controlling and regulating. Their life is goal-oriented. They want to move toward closure, even when the data are incomplete.

Perceiving types adapt well to changing situations. They make allowances for new information and for changes in the situation in which they are living or acting. They may have trouble making decisions, feeling that they have never quite got enough information on which to base their decision.

Perceiving types may start too many projects and consequently have difficulty in finishing them. They may tend to postpone unpleasant tasks and to give their attention to more pleasant options. Perceiving types want to know all about a new task before they begin it, and may prefer to postpone something while they continue to explore the options.

When perceiving types use lists they do so not as a way of organizing the details of their day, but as a way of seeing the possibilities in front of them. They may choose never to act on these possibilities. Perceiving types do not mind leaving things open for last-minute changes. They work best under pressure and get a lot accomplished at the last minute under the constraints of a deadline.

When individuals take a perceiving attitude toward the outer world, they are using the preferred *perceiving process*, sensing or intuition, outwardly. They are taking in information, adapting and changing, curious and interested. They adopt an open-minded attitude toward life and resist closure to obtain more data.

If, having read these contrasting descriptions, you are still puzzled about your real preferences between judging and perceiving, a very good test is to examine how you react best under pressure or when you are tired. Judging and perceiving types react in very different ways. Once again it is your less preferred function which is most likely to let you down.

For judging types it is the less preferred function of perceiving which lets them down when they are tired or under pressure. When tired, judging types become less flexible and more rigid. They are unable to respond to new challenges and panic about their ability to achieve things on time. A good example is when judging types are asked to make a public presentation at short notice, even about something on which they are well skilled. Judging types begin to make lists of what needs to be prepared, despair that there is insufficient time to get everything organized, and freeze in panic. For perceiving types, on the other hand, an invitation given at the last minute provides the very pressure needed for a good presentation.

For perceiving types it is the less preferred function of judging which lets them down when they are tired or under pressure. When tired, perceiving types become more difficult to pin down, more elusive when decisions are required, and more reluctant to engage in realistic planning. A good example is when perceiving types are asked to plan an event months before it is due to take place. Somehow perceiving types are completely unable to think ahead, to anticipate what is needed, and to make the essential arrangements well in advance. It is not until the last minute that everything begins to fall into place and others are expected to comply. For judging types, on the other hand, an invitation to plan well in advance provides the very structure and framework needed for a good presentation.

Given such a fundamental difference between judging and perceiving types, it is not surprising that they can sometimes easily misunderstand each other. On the one hand, judging types may experience perceiving types as people who are downright disorganized, messy and even irresponsible in their approach to life. On the other hand, perceiving types may experience judging types as people who are too demanding, rigid, inflexible and uptight. The truth of the matter is that judging and perceiving types deal with the world in very different ways.

Assessing psychological type

Having reviewed our definitions of the two orientations (extraversion and introversion), the two perceiving processes (sensing and intuition), the two judging processes (thinking and feeling) and the two attitudes toward the outer world (judging and perceiving), readers should now be in a good position to take an informed view of their own psychological type preferences. The result will be a sequence of four letters which can be located within the conventional type table displayed in Table 1.

Table 1: Type table

ISTJ	ISFJ	INFJ	INTJ
ISTP	ISFP	INFP	INTP
ESTP	ESFP	ENFP	ENTP
ESTJ	ESFJ	ENFJ	ENTJ

Within this type table, one of the authors of this book (Leslie) emerges as INTJ, indicating that he has preferences for introversion, intuition, thinking and judging. The other author (Andrew) emerges with a similar profile, differing by only one letter, INFJ, indicating that he has preferences for introversion, intuition, feeling and judging. We work together very well, both preferring to think things though on our own (introversion) before discussing our ideas with each other. We are both creative and imaginative people (intuition) who like to link ideas in new ways, and hence our novel insights into the relationship between biblical hermeneutics and psychological type theory. We are both people who like to have things organized and structured in our outer world (judging), and hence the fairly tight structure and pattern of this book. Where we differ, however, concerns our preferred way of evaluation. Leslie prefers thinking, while Andrew prefers feeling. This leads to some interesting differences in the ways we deal with problems and difficulties encountered with institutions and with people.

Now it is time for readers to pause and to reflect on what they have learnt about their own psychological type preferences.

While it is possible and sensible to form a good idea of one's own type preference by reflection on the basic theory, it is also helpful to complete a recognized measure of psychological type and to reflect on the feedback that comes from such an exercise. Probably the best known and most successfully marketed of the tools designed for assessing psychological type is the Myers-Briggs Type Indicator (MBTI) as developed by Myers and McCaulley (1985), Myers, McCaulley, Quenk and Hammer (1998) and Kendall (1998). Use of the Myers-Briggs Type Indicator is very professionally controlled, so that this instrument can only be purchased, administered and interpreted by practitioners who are properly qualified and registered for its application. Readers who want to learn more about their type preferences are strongly recommended to receive feedback from a qualified Myers-Briggs Type Indicator practitioner.

However, the Myers-Briggs Type Indicator is not the only instrument which has been designed to assess Jung's original notion of psychological type. The second best known instrument is probably the Keirsey Temperament Sorter (KTS) proposed by Keirsey and Bates (1978) and revised by Keirsey (1998). The most up-to-date version of this instrument is published in Keirsey's (1998) book *Please Understand Me: 2* and can also be found online. Other instruments designed to enable various adaptations of Jung's original notion of psychological type include the Gray-Wheelwright Jungian Type Survey (Gray and Wheelwright, 1946), the Singer-Loomis Inventory of Personality (Loomis, 1982), the Personality Style Inventory (Ware, Yokomoto and Morris, 1985), the Type Differentiation Indicator (Mitchell, 1991), the Cambridge Type Inventory (Rawling, 1992), the PET Type Check (Cranton and Knoop, 1995), the Jung Type Indicator (Budd, 1997), and the Personal Preferences Self-Description Questionnaire (Kier, Melancon and Thompson, 1998). The most recent instrument to be added to this growing family of tests is the Francis Psychological Type Scales (FPTS) developed by Francis (2005).

The Francis Psychological Type Scales are printed in the Appendix in order to help the readers of this book provide a further self-assessment of their psychological type and to allow the responses to this questionnaire to dialogue with the self-assessment made in the course of reading the descriptions of psychological type offered earlier in the chapter.

Type dynamics

A complete and proper introduction to Jungian psychological type theory also requires reference to what is known as 'type dynamics'. Type dynamics allows a great deal more to be read from the combination of the four letters than can be read from listening to the four choices independently.

The two processes concerned with perceiving or perception (sensing and intuition) and with judging or evaluation (thinking and feeling) stand at the heart of Jung's model of psychological type. According to the theory we need to be able to access all four functions in order to be balanced human beings. However, we develop these functions to different degrees. Of the two letters that we have chosen (S or N and T or F) one will have emerged as our strongest or *dominant* function and the other as our second strongest or *auxiliary* function.

It is the development of the dominant function which shapes the person we become and who is recognized by others, once they really get to know us. The dominant sensing type is the practical person, who is concerned with making things work. The dominant intuitive type is the ideas person, who is concerned with shaping things for the future. The dominant feeling type is the people-oriented person, who is concerned with caring for individuals. The dominant thinking type is the systems-orientated person, who is concerned with the integrity of the organization or the coherence of the theory.

The dominant function operates differently for introverts and for extraverts. For each, the dominant function works in the preferred world. So for the extravert the dominant function operates in the outside world, while the auxiliary function operates in the inside world. For the introvert the dominant function operates in the inside world, while the auxiliary function operates in the outside world. This is one of the reasons why introverts are more difficult to get to know quickly. What we meet first in the outside world is the introvert's second or auxiliary function. It takes longer to recognize the real strength of the dominant function at work in the inside world.

To complete the story of type dynamics we need to recognize the roles of the other two functions, the tertiary function and the inferior function. The tertiary function is the opposite pair of the auxiliary function.

The inferior function is the opposite pair of the dominant function. All this is best grasped through a concrete example.

One of the authors (Leslie) is an INTJ. We will now 'read' his type profile. The first step is to look at the last of the four letters. This tells us that he prefers to use a judging function in the outside world (J). Next we turn attention to the letter that expresses his judging preference. In this case his preference between thinking and feeling is thinking (T). So we now know that Leslie employs thinking in the outside world. When people first meet him they are inclined to see a logical and systematic person concerned with abstract principles rather than with interpersonal relationships. He can appear objective, critical and somewhat sceptical. Next we turn attention to the first letter which describes his preferred orientation. From this we learn that he is an introvert and that, therefore, the function we meet in the outside world is not Leslie's dominant, but his auxiliary function. The picture is completed by looking at the remaining letter concerned with the preferred perceiving process. Here we learn that Leslie's auxiliary thinking function is supported by the dominant intuitive function (N), which as an introvert he employs in his inside world. When you get to know him, you begin to see that his real strength resides in a somewhat playful creativity that is generating all sorts of possibilities. For Leslie the task of the auxiliary function (T) is to sort out these ideas generated in the inner world by the intuitive function (N) and to organize them in an acceptable way to present to the outside world.

This story now needs to be repeated for each of the remaining fifteen psychological types. That, however, is a task left over for another book. Sufficient has been written to indicate the potential within the theory for understanding self and others.

Conclusion

This chapter (together with the Appendix) has provided an introduction to psychological type theory. It has, however, done more than this by inviting the readers to step right inside the theory and to begin to develop an understanding of their own individual psychological type preferences. It is this inward psychological journey which is so crucial to understanding and to appreciating the SIFT method of biblical hermeneutics and liturgical preaching. Against this background, the next chapter turns attention to the research evidence linking psychological type to broader individual differences in religious expression.

Chapter 10

Psychological Type and Faith

Introduction

The previous chapter has provided a broad introduction to Jungian psychological type theory in order to establish the framework for the scientific psychology of hermeneutics advanced in this book. Against this background the aim of this chapter is to outline the broader research context within which the SIFT method of biblical hermeneutics and liturgical preaching has been developed. There are three main components to this broader context: research concerned with the psychological type profiling of religious professionals; research concerned with the psychological type profiling of church congregations; and research concerned with exploring the connection between psychological type and different ways of being religious. Each of these three components will be examined in turn.

Profiling religious professionals

A series of recent studies has begun to examine the psychological type characteristics of religious professionals. The first study in this series was reported by Francis, Payne and Jones (2001) drawing on data provided by 427 male Anglican clergy in Wales. The data demonstrated clear preferences for introversion over extraversion, for sensing over intuition, for feeling over thinking, and for judging over perceiving. The two predominant types were ISFJ (20 per cent) and ESFJ (13 per cent). Commenting on the implications of these findings for ministry in the Church in Wales, Francis, Payne and Jones (2001) made the following four points.

First, 59 per cent of the clergy preferred introversion, compared with 42 per cent who preferred extraversion. Introverts may bring many strengths to ministry, including the ability to work by themselves on tasks, to invest time in reading and in preparation, to welcome one-to-one encounters in counselling and in spiritual direction, to develop an inward life of prayer and spirituality. On the other hand, introverts may be drained by many of the social expectations of ministry, working with large groups of people, remembering names, visiting strangers and assuming a high profile in the local congregation and the wider local community.

Second, 57 per cent of the clergy preferred sensing, compared with 43 per cent who preferred intuition. Sensers may bring many strengths to ministry, including a fine awareness of the environment in which they serve and of the church in which they lead worship, a concern for the detail within the services they conduct and for the facts on which judgements and choices are made. On the other hand, sensers may find it more difficulty to formulate a vision for their church's future, to welcome change and experimentation in liturgy, or to see new and imaginative solutions to old problems.

Third, 69 per cent of the clergy preferred feeling, compared with 31 per cent who preferred thinking. Feelers may bring many strengths to ministry, including the desire to affiliate with others, the gifts of empathy and sympathy, a commitment to harmony, a deep understanding of people and a respect for inter-personal values. On the other hand, feelers may find it more difficult to take tough decisions which affect other people's lives, to chair troublesome meetings, to be assertive on points of truth and justice, and to put other people in their place.

Fourth, 68 per cent of the clergy preferred judging, compared with 32 per cent who preferred perceiving. Judgers may bring many strengths to ministry, including the ability to organize their own lives, to organize the life of their parishes, to arrange services and events well in advance, to keep on top of administration and to manage local affairs. On the other hand, judgers may become too inflexible and restricted by their own strategies, plans and routines, too unwilling or unable to abandon their plans in order to respond to unexpected crises, emergencies or opportunities, too bound to the present structure to embrace new ideas and possibilities.

The Church in Wales is separated from the Church of England by a very porous boundary, although the policies and ethos of the two Churches are set in very different contexts. Francis, Craig, Whinney, Tilley and Slater (2007) drew on data provided by 626 male Anglican clergy in England. In three ways these data reflected the same preferences as those found among male Anglican clergy in Wales: preferences for introversion over extraversion, for feeling over thinking, and for judging over perceiving. In one crucial way, however, the profiles of the two groups of clergymen differed. In Wales 57 per cent preferred sensing and 43 per cent preferred intuition; in England the balance was reversed, with 62 per cent preferring intuition and 38 per cent preferring sensing. Francis, Craig, Whinney, Tilley and Slater (2007) suggested that these differences in psychological type reflect a crucial difference in leadership styles between the two Churches and in the character of the two Churches. The Church in Wales tends to be more conservative than the Church of England and, therefore, a place in which leaders who prefer sensing may feel more comfortable. They suggested that clergymen who prefer intuition may become restless and impatient in the Church in Wales and cross the border to England, while clergymen who prefer sensing may become restless in the Church of England and cross the border into the Anglophone parts of Wales.

The two studies by Francis, Payne and Jones (2001) and Francis, Craig, Whinney, Tilley and Slater (2007) both drew attention to the high proportions of feelers among male clergy: 69 per cent in Wales and 54 per cent in England, compared with 35 per cent of men in the general population as reported by Kendall (1998). This finding is consistent with the view that the churches in the United Kingdom have become highly feminized communities (Brown, 2001) and that feeling characterizes a feminized approach to life. According to Kendall (1998) 70 per cent of women in the United Kingdom population prefer feeling. Such an analysis provides an important clue regarding why the churches may experience such difficulty in attracting individuals with a preference for thinking in general and in attracting men in particular.

A further study among 79 Roman Catholic priests reported by Craig, Duncan and Francis (2006a) also found a clear preference for feeling (79 per cent) over thinking (22 per cent). However, a series of studies conducted among evangelical church leaders, in comparison with Anglican and Catholic church leaders, found a higher proportion of thinkers. For example, preference for thinking was found among 56 per cent of the 81 male evangelical seminarians studied by Francis, Craig and Butler (2007), by 54 per cent of the 164 male church leaders studied by Craig, Francis and Robbins (2004) at the evangelical Spring Harvest, by 50 per cent of the 278 male Bible College students studied by Francis, Penson and Jones (2001), by 56 per cent of the 190 male Assemblies of God Bible College students studied by Kay, Francis and Craig (in press), by 52 per cent of the 130 male evangelical lay church leaders studied by Francis, Craig, Horsfall and Ross (2005), by 62 per cent of 42 male vergers studied by Craig, Duncan and Francis (2006b) and by 70 per cent of the 92 male evangelical missionary personnel studied by Craig, Horsfall and Francis (2005). Taken together, these findings suggest that there may be more opportunities for men who prefer thinking within leadership roles in evangelical churches, although this conclusion is qualified by Francis and Robbins' (2002) study of 57 male evangelical leaders, of whom just 44 per cent preferred thinking.

When compared with the population norms provided by Kendall (1998), there is a second way in which men engaged in Christian ministry differ from the profile of men in general. According to Kendall (1998), in the population as a whole just 27 per cent of men prefer intuition. Although the proportions of intuitives found in studies among men concerned with Christian ministry vary considerably from one group to another, in most groups they exceed the proportion within the general population. The highest proportion of intuitives is found in the study by Francis, Craig, Whinney, Tilley and Slater (2007) among 626 Church of England clergymen (62 per cent). Then, in descending order, intuitives accounted for: 49 per cent in the study by Craig, Duncan and Francis (2006a) among 79 Roman Catholic priests; 43 per cent in the study by Francis, Payne and Jones (2001) among 427 Anglican clergymen in Wales; 34 per cent in the study by Francis, Penson and Jones (2001) among 278 male students in an Evangelical Bible College; and 26 per cent in the study by Kay, Francis and Craig (in press) among 190 male students in a Pentecostal Bible College.

Three studies in this series also provided data on the psychological type profile of women engaged in or training for Christian ministry. The main conclusion from these three studies is that, like male church leaders, female church leaders are more likely to prefer intuition than is the case among women in the general population. According to Kendall (1998) in the general population just 21 per cent of women prefer intuition. In a study of 237 Anglican clergywomen in England, 65 per cent preferred intuition (Francis, Craig, Whinney, Tilley and Slater, 2007); in a study of 213 female students in an Evangelical Bible College, 34 per cent preferred intuition (Francis, Penson and Jones, 2001); and in a study of 122 female students in a Pentecostal Bible College, 38 per cent preferred intuition (Francis and Kay, in press). These data are considerably more limited in terms of quantity compared with the data available on male church leaders, simply because the full recognition of women into ordained ministry has only occurred quite recently in some denominations (for example, Anglicanism) and remains excluded by some other denominations (for example, Roman Catholicism).

The finding that the vocation to Christian ministry among both women and men attracts higher proportions of intuitives than are in the population as a whole, deserves considered reflection. On the one hand, there is the practical gospel of pastoral care which may be attractive to the pragmatic concerns of individuals with a preference for sensing. Here are the people responding to the call to feed the hungry, to clothe the naked, to visit the sick and to tend the dying. On the other hand, there is much more to the Christian gospel than the practice of good works in the here and now. The Christian gospel holds out a vision for the future, and faith in the future proclaims the unseen and the intangible. Here is a vision which may be grasped more easily by intuitives than by sensers. The Christian gospel continually challenges its adherents to work for change, to build a better future and to transform existing structures. Here are challenges which may be welcomed more easily by intuitives than by sensers.

In another study in this series, Francis, Nash, Nash and Craig (2007) examined the psychological type profile of 155 male and 134 female professional Christian youth ministers. This group emerged as significantly more extraverted than ministers in general and significantly less judging than ministers in general. These findings are interpreted to illuminate some of the tensions between Christian youth ministers and other members of the ministry team.

Profiling church congregations

A second series of recent studies has begun to examine the psychological type characteristics of church congregations. Three exploratory studies in this series were reported by Craig, Francis, Bailey and Robbins (2003), Francis, Duncan, Craig and Luffman (2004) and Francis, Robbins, Williams and Williams (2007) drawing on samples of 101, 327 and 185 churchgoers respectively. The third of these studies specifically compared the profile of male and female churchgoers with the population norms provided by Kendall (1998). The main finding from this comparison concerned the undue weighting toward sensing, feeling and judging in church congregations. Among women, ISFJ accounts for 32 per cent of churchgoers, compared with 18 per cent of the general population (P<.001), and ESFJ accounts for 28 per cent of churchgoers, compared with 19 per cent of the general population (P<.01). Among men, ISFJ accounts for 19 per cent of churchgoers, compared with 7 per cent of the general population (P<.001), and ESFJ accounts for 27 per cent of churchgoers, compared with 6 per cent of the general population (P<.001). Over-representation of ISFJ and ESFJ among churchgoers leads to under-representation of other types.

Commenting on these findings, Francis, Robbins, Williams and Williams (2007) argued that analysis of the more visible demographic characteristics of rural Anglican churchgoers (in terms of sex and age) suggests that, although the invitation of welcome may be issued indiscriminately to both sexes and to all ages, women are more likely to respond than men and the post-retired are more likely to respond than the pre-retired. Analysis of the less visible psychological characteristics of churchgoers (in terms of the 16 discrete psychological types) has also suggested that, although the invitation of welcome may be issued to all psychological types, individuals with a type preference for SFJ are more likely to respond than individuals with other type preferences.

In her booklet, *Introduction to Type*, Myers (1998, p. 7) provides insightful profiles of the two SFJ types: ISFJ and ESFJ. The ISFJ profile is as follows:

> Quiet, friendly, responsible and conscientious. Work devotedly to meet their obligations. Lend stability to any project or group. Thorough, painstaking, accurate. Their interests are usually not technical. Can be patient with necessary details. Loyal, considerate, perceptive, concerned with how other people feel.

The ESFJ profile is as follows:

> Warm-hearted, talkative, popular, conscientious, born co-operators, active committee members. Need harmony and may be good at creating it. Always doing something nice for someone. Work best with encouragement and praise. Main interest is in things that directly and visibly affect people's lives.

There are important ways in which these two profiles describe the kind of people we might expect to have responded to the call of welcome to join church congregations. The SFJ congregations possess a number of recognizable Christian strengths. The preference for feeling (F) characterizes a community concerned with human values, interpersonal relationships and with a loving and caring God. Here is a community concerned with peace and with harmony. The population norms show that feeling is a feminine preference *par excellence* (reported by 70 per cent of women and by 35 per cent of men). A community shaped by such a dominant preference for feeling may, however, be quite alien to individuals who view the world through the lens of thinking (including the majority of men). Thinkers, too, may desire to respond to the call of Christ, but this response may appear quite different from the response of feelers.

The preference for sensing (S) characterizes a community concerned with continuity, tradition, stability, and with a God grounded in divine changelessness. Here is a community concerned with guarding what has been handed down by previous generations. The population norms show that sensing is the preferred mode of the British population (reported by 79 per cent of women and by 73 per cent of men). In this sense, the church congregation is in step with wider society. A community shaped by such a dominant preference for sensing may, however, be quite alien to individuals who view the world through the lens of intuition. Intuitives, too, may desire to respond to the call of Christ, but this response may appear quite different from the response of sensers.

The preference for judging (J) characterizes a community concerned with organization, discipline, structure, and with a God who welcomes a regular pattern to worship (whatever that pattern may be). Here is a community concerned with valuing regular commitment, advanced planning and respect for the guidelines (implicit as well as explicit). The population norms show that judging is the preferred mode of the British population (reported by 62 per cent of women and by 55 per cent of men). In this sense, the church congregation is once again in step with wider society. A community shaped by such a dominant preference for judging may, however, be quite alien to individuals who view the world through the lens of perceiving. Perceivers, too, may desire to respond to the call of Christ, but this response may appear quite different from the response of judgers.

Building on this tradition, Village, Francis and Craig (in press) in a study of 290 churchgoers found significant differences in type profiles between individuals attending evangelical Anglican churches and individuals attending Anglo-Catholic churches. There was a significantly higher proportion of intuitives in the Anglo-Catholic congregations. In a study of 2,658 churchgoers, Craig (2005) found significant differences in type profiles between individuals attending rural and urban churches.

There was a significantly higher proportion of sensers in rural congregations.

Other studies in this tradition have reported on the psychological type profiles of 93 female and 65 male active members of the Anglican Church (Francis, Butler, Jones and Craig, 2007), 246 male and 380 female participants in Christian programmes (Craig, Francis and Barwick, in press), 74 female and 40 male members of Anglican church councils (Francis, Butler and Craig, 2005), 104 student members of a university-based Christian Union (Craig, Bigio, Robbins and Francis, 2005), 79 female churchgoers (Craig, Williams, Francis and Robbins, 2006) and 30 volunteer workers in a rural Christian charity shop (Francis and Pegg, 2007). These studies generally confirm the strong SFJ preference in Christian communities. The study of the volunteer workers in the Christian charity shop showed a strong preference for extraversion, in contrast with the general preference for introversion among churchgoers. Francis and Pegg (2007) concluded from this finding that activities like the Christian charity shop may provide a focus of interest for those extraverted members of the community who may feel less at home in the normal introverted church congregation.

Different ways of being religious

A third series of recent studies has begun to examine the power of psychological type theory to predict individual differences in religiosity. Five different strands of research have been initiated within this context.

The first strand has examined the connection between psychological type and attitude toward Christianity, building on the well-established research tradition which had documented a stable link between attitude toward Christianity and the three-dimensional model of personality proposed by Hans Eysenck (Francis, Lewis, Brown, Philipchalk and Lester, 1995), using the Francis Scale of Attitude toward Christianity (Francis, Lewis, Philipchalk, Brown and Lester, 1995). The four studies in this series have been based on samples of 82 students (Jones and Francis, 1999), 367 students (Fearn, Francis and Wilcox, 2001), 149 students (Francis, Robbins, Boxer, Lewis, McGuckin and McDaid, 2003), and 552 students (Francis, Jones and Craig, 2004). The findings from these four studies are inconclusive and suggest that all types may come to faith, but in somewhat different ways.

The second strand has examined the connection between psychological type and mystical orientation, drawing on the conceptualization and measurement proposed by Francis and Louden (2000a) in the Mystical Orientation Scale. The three studies in this series have been based on samples of 100 students and adult churchgoers (Francis and Louden, 2000b), 543 participants attending workshops concerned with personality and spirituality (Francis, 2002), and 318 individuals who frequented the retreat house associated with Ampleforth Abbey (Francis, Village, Robbins and Ineson, 2007). The most secure conclusion to emerge from these studies is that mystical orientation is associated with the perceiving process: intuitives are more open than sensers to mystical orientation. This finding is consistent with the earlier finding of Francis and Ross (1997) among 379 participants attending spirituality courses that sensers record higher scores than intuitives on an index of traditional Christian spirituality, while intuitives record higher scores than sensers on an index of experiential spirituality. Francis and Ross (1997) argued that the recognition of different preferences between sensers and intuitives may help to explain some conflicting experiences between clergy and congregations. For example, worship leaders who have a clear preference for intuition may find it difficult to understand why their attempts to provide more creative or experientially based forms of worship are so strongly resisted by congregations which have a clear preference for sensing.

The third strand has examined the connection between psychological type and charismatic experience, building on an earlier set of studies concerned with locating charismatic experience within Eysenck's three-dimensional model of personality (Francis and Thomas, 1997; Robbins, Hair and Francis, 1999; Louden and Francis, 2001; Francis and Robbins, 2003). These earlier studies tended to show that charismatic experience was associated with high extraversion scores and with low neuroticism scores. The two studies examining the connection between psychological type and charismatic experience were based on samples of 36 committed Christian adults (Francis and Jones, 1997) and 925 Christian adults attending workshops on personality and spirituality (Jones, Francis and Craig, 2005). The data demonstrate that, compared with non-charismatics, the charismatic sample contains significantly higher proportions of extraverts, thinkers and perceivers. Compared with the non-charismatic sample, there is a significantly higher proportion of dominant thinkers among the charismatic sample. Among the charismatic sample there is a significant over-representation of ESTJ and a significant under-representation of ISFJ.

The fourth strand has examined the connection between psychological type and different styles of religious believing. The first study in this series examined the relationship between scores recorded on an index of conservative Christian belief and psychological type preferences among a sample of 315 adult churchgoers (Francis and Jones, 1998). The data demonstrated that Christians who preferred sensing and thinking were more likely to hold traditional beliefs than Christians who preferred intuition and feeling. In a second study drawing on the same database, Francis and Jones (1999) examined the relationship between psychological type and tolerance for religious uncertainty. The data demonstrated that Christians who preferred intuition rather than sensing were more tolerant of religious uncertainty. Taking this question one step further, Francis and Ross (2000) examined the relationship between psychological type and the Batson and Ventis six-item measure of quest orientation of religiosity (Batson and Ventis, 1982) among a sample of 64 active Catholic churchgoers. These data provided inconclusive results. The next study in the series, however, by Ross and Francis (in press) employed the quest measure proposed by the New Indices of Religious Orientation (Francis, 2007a) among a sample of 481 weekly-churchgoing Christians. These data confirmed a positive association between intuition and the quest orientation of religiosity.

Psychological type and hermeneutics

Against the background of this third series of recent studies, Village and Francis (2005) designed an empirical study to examine the relationship between psychological type preferences and preferred ways for interpreting scripture. The survey instrument used in this study invited participants to read the passage from Mark 9.14–29, concerning the healing of a boy possessed by an evil spirit. The text was printed from the New Revised Standard Version, but with book, chapter and verse annotations removed. Later in the survey instrument, short responses to the passage were presented in pairs, either reflecting a choice between the two perceiving processes (sensing and intuition) or between the two judging processes (thinking and feeling). The study participants were asked in each case to identify which one of the two responses more clearly reflected their own response to the passage from scripture. For example, in terms of the perceiving process, participants were invited to choose between 'This story is a vivid account of a healing that speaks for itself' (intended to reflect sensing) and 'This story raises questions about the nature of sickness and the power of prayer' (intended to reflect intuition). For example, in terms of the judging process, participants were invited to choose between 'The evidence suggests that the boy had epilepsy; though what matters is how it was perceived at the time' (intended to reflect thinking) and 'I feel sympathy for the boy, who must have been very frightened' (intended to reflect feeling).

It is important in this type of research that the interpretative items presented genuinely reflect characteristics likely to be attractive to the relevant type. There is no objective way of producing items, so items were tested in two pilot trials and accepted only if they appeared to discriminate between the relevant types. In addition, all the items used in the final questionnaire were tested *post priori*, using a sample of 21 experts in psychological type, such as Myers-Briggs Type Indicator practitioners. They were given all the individual items in random order and asked to indicate if they considered them responses that would be preferred by dominant S, N, F or Ts. All but four of the items were correctly assigned by at least 70 per cent of experts. This indicated that they were likely to assess the correct type.

Data provided by a sample of 404 lay adult Anglicans from eleven different churches confirmed a match between preferred biblical interpretation and psychological type preferences in both the perceiving (sensing versus intuition) and judging (feeling versus thinking) processes. The findings from this study, therefore, provided empirical support for the theoretical insights that had informed the SIFT method of biblical hermeneutics and liturgical preaching.

Conclusion

This chapter has described and discussed the growing body of empirical research evidence concerned with the relationship between psychological type and the Christian community. Four main conclusions can be distilled from the empirical evidence. First, it is important to recognize that neither church congregations nor religious professionals are fully representative of the distribution of psychological type preferences within the wider population. There appear to be strong tendencies toward self-selection within both congregations and Christian ministry. Such self-selection needs to be tested against a strong theological conviction that all are called and invited by a God who is committed to equality of opportunity. Second, it is important to recognize that there are important signs of variation and differences within the Christian community. Differences in religious provision appear to have the potential to embrace a broader range of psychological types within the

Christian community. Third, it is important to recognize that psychological type preferences seem to interact with ways in which scripture is heard, interpreted and applied. There are clear challenges, therefore, for the psychological science of hermeneutics to interact with and to inform the processes of biblical hermeneutics and liturgical preaching. Preachers who heed the dominical command to love the Lord their God with all their mind and with all their soul may well be in a stronger position both to hear and to interpret the voice of God within their community. It is this task that is now addressed more fully in the next chapter.

Chapter 11

Psychological Type and Preaching

Introduction

The preceding chapters in this part of the book began by establishing the theological case for taking individual differences seriously. We have argued that, properly understood, individual differences in personality reflect the intentionality of the divine creator. Then we examined the potential of three different psychological models of personality for illuminating individual differences within the Christian community. We have argued that different psychological models of personality are capable of serving the Christian community in different ways, but that the model of psychological type, as originally advanced by Carl Jung, is particularly pertinent for developing a fully rounded approach to biblical hermeneutics and liturgical preaching. This is the case because this model of personality embraces at its core an understanding of the two central mental processes of perception (perceiving) and evaluation (judging) as already identified in the first part of this book as core to an understanding of hermeneutics.

Against this background, the aim of this chapter is to set psychological type theory to work in the service of preaching. After the theory comes the practice. After the analysis comes the application. This chapter is concerned with the practice of preaching in the light of psychological type theory.

Although it is the two core processes of perceiving (sensing and intuition) and judging (feeling and thinking) that are key to the SIFT method of biblical hermeneutics and liturgical preaching, the orientations (extraversion and introversion) and the attitudes toward the outer world (judging and perceiving) also are of considerable relevance to the ways in which preachers set about their task. In this chapter, therefore, attention will be given to the orientations and to the attitudes toward the outer world before focusing on the perceiving processes and on the judging processes.

Introversion and extraversion

We need to begin by revisiting the description of the introvert and of the extravert offered in Chapter 9 and then we need to draw out the implications of these psychological preferences for understanding how introverted preachers and extraverted preachers may best go about their preparation for preaching.

On the one hand, introverts like quiet for concentration. They want to be able to shut off the distractions of the outer world and turn inwards. Introverts work best alone and may dislike distractions and interruptions from other people. Introverts prefer to learn by reading rather than by discussing with others. They are reflective people who probe inwardly for stimulation.

In order to engage fully and effectively with their ministry of preaching, introverted preachers need to be able to step back from the business of daily life and to create enough space and solitude to reflect on the text of scripture and on the context of the community among whom they will be preaching. For some, this may mean going into their own room and closing the door. For some, this may mean creating their own internal island of quiet on a busy train, in a busy street or in a crowded room. To be really creative, introverts need to feel that they can be immune from interruption and distraction. The thought of the telephone sitting on the desk ready to ring at any moment may distract the introvert from settling to the task. For the introverted preacher the stimulation for reflection comes from the books on the shelf and the ideas stored in the mind.

On the other hand, extraverts like variety and action. They like to have other people around them, and enjoy the stimulation of interruptions. Extraverts prefer to learn by talking things through with other people. They often find that their own ideas become clarified through communicating them with others. They are active people who scan the outer environment for stimulation.

In order to engage fully and effectively with this ministry of preaching, extraverted preachers need to be able to engage with others in order to talk about and to discuss the text of scripture and the context of the community among whom they will be preaching. For the extravert, sitting in a quiet room may be disabling. For the extravert, being left alone with the pile of commentaries may be quite unproductive. To be really creative, extraverts need to feel that they can discuss their developing ideas with others and seek clarification though dialogue and conversation. Extraverts would rather address their questions by asking others than by searching through reference books. A proper understanding of their own psychological type preferences may encourage a group of extraverted preachers to meet in order to discuss their sermon preparation. Or they may agree to speak by telephone as they recognize the need to draw on each other's support.

Psychological insight into the differences between introverts and extraverts makes it clear that there may be no one right way in which to prepare for preaching, but that there are different ways in which extraverts and introverts may do so more effectively. The difficulty, however, arises when introverted preachers try to teach extraverts to do things the introverted way, or vice versa.

It is also important to recognize how the distinctive characteristics of introversion and of extraversion bring both strengths and weaknesses to preaching. The introvert's preference for learning through reading and for quiet, reflective solitary study may bring to the pulpit good familiarity with the text, with the commentaries, with the views of recognized theologians, or engagement with wider literature. The introvert may, however, have spent less time interacting with and engaging with the local community. Preaching may be less rooted in the immediate experiences of local people. The extravert's preference for learning through experience, social engagement and interaction with others may bring to the pulpit good familiarity with the concerns of the local community and with the lives of local people. The extravert may, however, have spent less time engaging with the biblical text and with the insights of scholars. Returning to the distinction refined in Part 1 of this book, introverts may be better at reading the text than reading the context, while extraverts may be better at reading the context than reading the text.

Judging and perceiving

We need to begin by revisiting the descriptions of judging and perceiving offered in Chapter 9 and then we need to draw out the implications of these psychological preferences for understanding how judging preachers and perceiving preachers may best go about their preparation for preaching.

On the one hand, individuals who prefer to relate to the outer world with a judging process present a planned and orderly approach to life. They prefer to have a settled system in place and display a preference for closure. Judging types schedule projects so that each step gets done on time. They work best when they can plan their work in advance and then follow that plan. Judging types tend to be satisfied when they have finished what they set out to achieve. They dislike having to revise their decisions and having to take fresh information into account.

In order to engage fully and effectively with their ministry of preaching, judging preachers need to be able to plan and to structure their preparation and then to be able to implement that framework. For some, this may mean structuring sermon preparation into the plan for the whole week. There are some judging preachers who may follow the discipline of studying the text on Monday, relating the text to the local context on Tuesday, and writing out the whole sermon on Wednesday. That task completed, it is now possible to choose the hymns, to design the posters and to organize participation well in advance. There are other judging preachers who may plan a whole course of sermons weeks in advance and have everything ready and planned in the file for a whole sequence of Sundays well ahead of schedule.

On the other hand, individuals who prefer to relate to the outer world with a perceiving process present a flexible and spontaneous approach to life. They prefer to keep plans and organizations to a minimum and display a preference for openness. Perceiving types adapt well to changing situations. They make allowances for new information and for changes in the situations in which they are living or acting. Perceiving types do not mind leaving things open for last-minute changes. They work best under pressure and get a lot accomplished at the last minute under the constraints of a deadline.

In order to engage fully and effectively with their ministry of preaching, perceiving preachers need to be able to keep their options open for as long as possible. For some this may mean reflecting on many different passages of scripture during the course of the week, collecting and reflecting on apparently unrelated experiences and ideas, and resisting choosing the hymns and selecting the music until as late as possible. Perceiving preachers need the pressures that build up late on Saturday evening or early on Sunday morning before everything really begins to fall into place.

Psychological insight into the differences between judgers and perceivers makes it clear that there may be no one right way in which to prepare for preaching, but that there are different ways in which judgers and perceivers may do so more effectively. The difficulty, however, arises when preachers who prefer judging try to teach perceivers to do things the judging way, or vice versa.

It is also important to recognize how the distinctive characteristics of judging and of perceiving bring both strengths and weaknesses to preaching. The judging preacher's preference for having things well planned, organized and prepared in advance may bring to the pulpit a sense of discipline and preparation. On the other hand, their preaching may lack the sense of immediacy and spontaneity. It is preachers like these who may find it very difficult to produce a good sermon on the spur of the moment, to fill a gap at the last minute when a colleague falls sick, or to respond to an unexpected crisis in parish life or in world politics. The perceiving preacher's preference for keeping things open and flexible to the last minute may bring to the pulpit a sense of immediacy, spontaneity and engagement with topical issues and recent experiences. On the other hand, their preaching may lack the sense of organization, depth and clarity. It is preachers like these who may find it very difficult to co-ordinate a worship team that presses for decisions in advance, like readers who want to prepare the readings, musicians who want to practise the music, and intercessors who want to link with the central theme of the preacher.

Sensing and intuition

We need to begin by revisiting the descriptions of sensing and intuition offered in Chapter 9 and then we need to draw out the implications of these psychological preferences for understanding how sensing and intuitive preachers go about their preparation for preaching. Returning to ideas established and discussed in Part 1 of this book, this discussion of sensing and intuition re-engages our concern with the role of perception in hermeneutics, since according to the Jungian model of the human psyche sensing and intuition comprise the two functions of the perceiving process. So how do sensing preachers and intuitive preachers differ in the ways in which they read the Bible, read the Spirit and read the context?

On the one hand, individuals who prefer sensing have a keen interest in what is there in front of them. When they confront the passage of scripture on which they intend to preach, their first response is to savour the details in the text, to find out all they can about that text and to know well what it is saying. This may mean cross-referencing the passage with other parts of the Bible, looking at what the commentaries have to say about the meanings of the words, and setting the passage in its proper historical and cultural context. This basic and fundamental research they will want to share with their listeners.

Sensing types have a keen eye for detail. When they are reading the local, the national or the international context into which they are preaching, their first response is to make sure that they have got their facts right. They will assemble the evidence and the information from the variety of sources that come to hand. This may mean listening to the evidence offered by local people, giving close attention to the national media, or searching the internet for facts and information.

Sensing types are cautious about over-interpreting the evidence in front of them and about drawing far-reaching conclusions that may stretch beyond the available data. When they are reading the Spirit, seeking evidence of God's activity in the world, they may prefer conventional signs of God's activity which are consistent with the main perspectives of their own interpretative community. Sensing types may be reluctant to claim that their God is doing a new thing.

On the other hand, individuals who prefer intuition have the ability to cut through a mass of detail to see a clear pattern or an emerging theme. When they confront the passage of scripture on which they intend to preach, their first response is to focus on one distinctive aspect of the narrative and to identify a big theme or a major issue behind that distinctive aspect. Rather than concentrate on the details of the passage itself, the intuitive preacher will begin to link the emerging theme with other sources of inspiration to develop that theme further. This may mean linking the passage with very diverse parts of scripture, with ideas running through literature or with current themes illustrated by television, films or other sources of inspiration. For the intuitive, the big theme is so much more important than the minutiae of the text.

Intuitive types have a good sense of how things may develop or where things will lead. When they are reading the local, the national or the international context into which they are preaching, their first response is to try to grasp the big overall picture. They probably will have neither time nor interest to sort through the facts and evidence, but they will be interested in hearing the commentators who speculate about what it all means or where it is all going. This may mean taking a particular or distinctive interpretative view on what is happening and then trying to interpret whatever evidence comes to hand through the lens of that interpretation.

Intuitive types tend to trust their own hunches and insights. When they are reading the Spirit, seeking evidence of God's activity in the world, they may be willing to come to bold conclusions, to develop a visionary or prophetic stand, and to offer novel interpretations of the evidence. Intuitive types may be all too ready to claim that their God is doing a new thing.

Psychological insight into the differences between sensers and intuitives makes it clear that there may be no one right way in which to go about the crucial hermeneutical task of perception, but that there are different insights that sensers and intuitives may bring to the hermeneutical process through the highly distinctive ways in which they read the Bible, read the Spirit and read the context. The difficulty, however, arises when sensing preachers try to insist that intuitives do things the sensing way, or vice versa.

It is important to recognize how the distinctive characteristics of sensing and intuition bring both strengths and weaknesses to the hermeneutical process of perception. The sensing types' preference for facts and details may bring to the pulpit a wealth of information and carefully recorded evidence about the text of scripture and about the contemporary world. The senser may, however, have failed to grasp and to identify the major themes and bigger pictures to which the text points. The intuitive types' preferences for seeing links and possibilities may bring to the pulpit a well-developed reflection for which the text of scripture was the essential springboard. Yet, by the time the sermon is preached, the text itself may have been well and truly submerged, if not totally forgotten. The intuitive may lose touch with the evidence, being so caught up in the interpretation.

Thinking and feeling

We need to begin by revisiting the descriptions of thinking and feeling offered in Chapter 9 and then we need to draw out the implications of these psychological preferences for understanding how thinking and feeling preachers go about their preparation for preaching. Returning to ideas established and discussed in Part 1 of this book, this discussion of thinking and feeling re-engages our concern with the role of evaluation in hermeneutics, since according to the Jungian model of the human psyche thinking and feeling comprise the two functions of the judging (or evaluating) process. So how do thinking preachers and feeling preachers differ in the ways in which they read the Bible, read the Spirit and read the context?

On the one hand, individuals who prefer feeling have a keen interest in the human and interpersonal aspects and implications of what is there in front of them. When they confront the passage of scripture on which they intend to preach, their first response is to consider the impact on human life. For some, this will mean entering an empathic relationship with characters in the narrative, walking in their shoes and experiencing how it felt for them. Their concern is to identify with the human story, to identify with the human motivation, and to appreciate the personal and inter-personal values at the heart of the decision-making and evaluative processes.

Feeling types have a keen eye for the inter-personal issues at stake in situations. When they are reading the local, the national or the international context into which they are preaching, their first response is to ask how people's lives are being affected and how decisions and evaluations will impact on the human experience and on the human situation. This may mean getting alongside local people to share in their experience, or trying to experience the motivation of national or international figures caught up in current activity or action.

Feeling types are passionately concerned with the quest for peace, harmony and reconciliation. When they are reading the Spirit, seeking evidence of God's activity in the world, they may be most ready to see God at work in acts of kindness, healing and restoration, bringing peace, wholeness and healing to a troubled world or to troubled individuals. Their antennae may be more attuned to the God of mercy than to the God of justice.

On the other hand, individuals who prefer thinking have a keen interest in the logical and theological aspects and implications of what is there in front of them. When they confront the passage of scripture on which they intend to preach, their first response is to consider the kind of truth claims being made, being raised or being tested. For some, this will mean placing the passage in the wider context of theological debate, while for others it will mean testing the theological coherence of the passage itself.

Thinking types have a keen eye for the issues of fairness, truth and justice at stake in situations. When they are reading the local, the national or the international context into which they are preaching, their first response is to identify the main principles that are at stake, and to establish how decisions and evaluations impact matters of principle. This may mean campaigning against injustice, inequality and unfairness. This may mean trying to mobilize the local church to take action on matters of local, national or international concern when fundamental human principles have been violated.

Thinking types are passionately concerned with the quest for truth, justice and fairness. When they are reading the Spirit, seeking evidence of God's activity in the world, they may be most ready to see God at work in acts of vindication, restoring justice, righting wrongs and upholding eternal truths. Their antennae may be more attuned to the God of justice than to the God of mercy.

Psychological insight into the differences between thinkers and feelers makes it clear that there may be no one right way in which to go about the crucial hermeneutical task of evaluation, but that there are different insights that thinkers and feelers may bring to the hermeneutical process through the highly distinctive ways in which they read the Bible, read the Spirit and read the context. The difficulty, however, arises when thinking preachers try to insist that feelers should do things the thinking way, or vice versa.

It is important to recognize how the distinctive characteristics of thinking and feeling bring both strengths and weaknesses to the hermeneutical process of evaluation. The thinking types' preference for matters of principle, for issues of truth and justice and for matters of logical and theological concern may bring to the pulpit an emphasis on theological teaching, a commitment to matters of principle and a gospel dominated by the God of justice. The thinker may, however, fail to appreciate some of the human implications of such teaching. Proclaiming an objective analysis of minor disputes within the local church may leave some members bruised, hurt and defiant. Out of proper concern for matters of principle, preachers who prefer thinking may hurt individuals. The feeling types' preference for seeing the personal and inter-personal dimensions of life may bring to the pulpit an emphasis on themes concerned with peace and harmony and a gospel dominated by the God of mercy. The feeler may, however, fail to grasp the pressing issues of truth and justice that also reflect the rounded message of the full gospel. Failing to grasp the nettle over minor disputes in the local church may leave unresolved issues debilitating the church for years to come. Out of proper concern for the peace and well-being of individuals, preachers who prefer feeling may hurt the institution.

Psychological type and hermeneutics

While the two orientations (introversion and extraversion) and the two attitudes toward the outer world (judging and perceiving) carry important implications for ways in which individual preachers prefer to prepare for preaching, the two perceiving processes (sensing and intuition) and the two judging processes (thinking and feeling) are actively involved in the hermeneutical process itself. According to psychological type theory, each preacher will have an innate preference for one of the perceiving functions (sensing or intuition) and for one of the judging functions (thinking or feeling).

Moreover, one of these two preferred functions (the preferred perceiving function or the preferred judging function) will be the stronger or the better developed. This is known as the dominant function, while the other preferred function is known as the auxiliary function. The function paired with the dominant function is the least developed of all and is known as the inferior function. The function paired with the auxiliary function is known as the tertiary function. This somewhat complex situation is best exemplified by a concrete example.

As already discussed in Chapter 9, the type preference for one of the authors of this book (Leslie) is INTJ. In this case the dominant function is intuition and the auxiliary function is thinking. As a consequence the inferior function is sensing (the opposite pair with intuition) and the tertiary function is feeling (the opposite pair with thinking). In the hermeneutical process Leslie feels most comfortable with the intuitive perspective and quite comfortable with the thinking perspective. He is less comfortable with the feeling perspective and least comfortable with the sensing perspective.

Thinking back now to his early and formative years as a preacher, Leslie recognizes that many of his sermons reflected his own preference for intuition and for thinking. There are three implications which follow from this recognition. The first implication is that there may be a tendency for preachers to nurture a congregation in their own image. Leslie may have been building a church that was particularly accessible to others who preferred dominant intuition with auxiliary thinking. The second implication is that sensers may find it difficult to identify with the perspective offered by intuitives, while feelers may find it difficult to identify with the perspective offered by thinkers. The third implication is the most important of all. Taking the psychology of hermeneutics seriously, we should not rest content with only a partial approach to the text. The dominical command to love the Lord our God with all our mind and with all our soul demands proper engagement of all four psychological functions.

Having looked at the issue through the eyes of the preacher, it is wise to examine the perspective of the listener. At its most basic level, the sensing type needs to respond to facts and information, to details and clearly defined images. The intuitive type needs to respond to challenges to the imagination and arresting ideas, to theories and possibilities. The feeling type needs to respond to issues of the heart and to the stuff of human relationships. The thinking type needs to respond to issues of the head and to the stuff of logical analysis.

Of course, left to their own devices preachers will emphasize their own type preference. The preacher who prefers intuition will preach a message full of fast-moving ideas and imaginative associations. The sensing types in the congregation will quickly lose the thread and accuse those preachers of having their heads in the air and their shoes high above the ground. The preacher who prefers sensing will preach a message full of detailed information and the close analysis of text. The intuitive types in the congregation will quickly tire of the detail and accuse those preachers of being dull and failing to see the wood for the trees.

The preacher who prefers feeling will preach a message full of human interest and of loving concern for people. The thinking types in the congregation will quickly become impatient with this emphasis on inter-personal matters and accuse those preachers of failing to grasp the hard intellectual issues and the pressing challenges and contradictions of the faith. The preacher who prefers thinking will preach a message full of theological erudition and carefully argued nuance of perspective. The feeling types in the congregation will quickly become impatient with this emphasis on theological abstraction and accuse those preachers of missing the very heart of the Gospel which cries out for compassion, understanding and human warmth.

Like preachers, listeners need to be encouraged by the psychological science of biblical hermeneutics to go beyond the perspective of their own psychological preferences to engage with the full richness of the text. It is for this reason that the SIFT method of biblical hermeneutics and liturgical preaching wants to hold out both to preacher and to listener a disciplined approach to addressing the text, moving through the perspectives of sensing, intuition, feeling and thinking. There is a logic in this order. We need the sensing function to ground us in the reality of the passage of scripture. We need the intuitive function to draw out the wider implications and to develop the links. We need the feeling function to become attuned to the issues of values and human priorities within the narrative. We need the thinking function to face the theological implications and to struggle with the intellectual issues.

Conclusion

This chapter has set out to examine the implications of psychological type theory for preaching and from the perspective of the preacher. By re-visiting the descriptions given in Chapter 9 of the two orientations (extraversion and introversion), the two perceiving processes (sensing and intuition), the two judging processes (thinking and feeling) and the two attitudes toward the outside world (judging and perceiving), important conclusions have been drawn regarding two areas: how preachers go about their task of preparing to preach and how preachers engage with the hermeneutical processes of perception and evaluation in reading the Bible, reading the Spirit and reading the context. The chapter has concluded by introducing the SIFT method of biblical hermeneutics and liturgical preaching as a way to engage with the full richness of the text, attending to the perspectives and insights afforded by all four psychological functions. It is the task of the next chapter to set this method to work.

Chapter 12

Psychological Type and Biblical Hermeneutics

Introduction

The previous chapter has reviewed the broad implications of psychological type theory for the hermeneutical process in general and for the specific engagement of preachers in their tasks of reading the Bible, reading the Spirit and reading the context. This chapter focuses these broad implications through a more detailed presentation and examination of the SIFT method of biblical hermeneutics and liturgical preaching. Attention is first given to the more abstract and theoretical consideration of the method, and then attention is turned to a specific worked example. Following the precedent established in Part 1 of this book, the passage chosen for the worked example of the SIFT method of biblical hermeneutics and liturgical preaching is once again Mark 4.35–41, the Stilling of the Storm.

Establishing the SIFT method

When the previous chapter examined the relevance of psychological type theory for the preacher, a clear distinction was made between two different issues. First, it was argued that the two orientations (introversion and extraversion) and the two attitudes (judging and perceiving) may be of central importance in understanding and interpreting individual differences in ways in which preachers set about their task of preparing sermons. Second, it was argued that the two perceiving processes (sensing and intuition) and the two judging processes (thinking and feeling) may be of central importance in understanding and interpreting individual differences in ways in which preachers (and people in general) engage with the fundamental hermeneutical tasks of

135

perception and evaluation when reading the Bible, reading the Spirit and reading the context. The case was then taken one step further to argue that a full and rounded interpretation demanded a hermeneutical process that engaged all four psychological processes (sensing, intuition, thinking and feeling).

At that stage in the argument, we introduced the SIFT method of biblical hermeneutics and liturgical preaching. Building on our interpretation of contemporary hermeneutical theory and psychological type theory, we have concluded that a full and rounded interpretation of scripture in general, and the four Gospels in particular, can best proceed by addressing the text in a systematic way through the four perspectives of sensing, intuition, feeling and thinking, taken in that order. In this way we are engaging the text in full dialogue with the human mind, unlocking the revelatory potential of the full engagement of God's Word with the human context and with the human condition, and being faithful to the dominical command to love the Lord our God with all our mind and with all our soul.

In the systematic application of psychological type theory to illuminate the process of hermeneutics, the SIFT method of biblical hermeneutics and liturgical preaching begins with the two perceiving processes (sensing and intuition) before proceeding to the two judging processes (thinking and feeling). This sequencing acknowledges that in the hermeneutical process perception properly precedes evaluation. In other words, information and ideas, data and theories have to be considered before evaluation takes place. In the systematic application of psychological type theory to illuminate the process of hermeneutics, there is also good reason why the SIFT method of biblical hermeneutics and liturgical preaching deals with sensing before intuition (the two processes concerned with perception) and deals with feeling before thinking (the two processes concerned with evaluation).

The SIFT method begins with sensing because the sensing function is concerned with ensuring that the evidence and the data have been properly observed and noted. The discipline of sensing ensures that the given passage of text has been properly located and situated. As far as readings from the four Gospels are concerned, it is important to note which evangelist is speaking and how the related passage fits into the overall structure of that Gospel. It is important to note, as part of the proper contextualization, how this particular evangelist may have treated the account differently from the other evangelists if there are parallels in other Gospels. For example, the sensing function would be sensitive to the ways in which Luke fails to repeat Mark's detailed account of John the Baptist's physical appearance and dress. The discipline of sensing ensures that the given passage is heard in its own voice and not confused with other accounts. For example, the sensing function would be sensitive to the way in which the divine voice at Jesus' baptism was addressed to Jesus in the second person singular in the Marcan account and not to the crowd. The discipline of sensing ensures that the echoes of the Old Testament redolent in the Gospels are properly pursued and checked out. For example, the sensing function would pursue the trail from Mark's account of John the Baptist's attire to the roots in 1 Kings where Elijah was recognized through his clothing made of camel's hair. Through such activities, the sensing function establishes the foundation on which the other functions can build.

The SIFT method brings the intuitive function into play *after* the sensing function because the big danger with the intuitive function is that it may fly off at a tangent far too easily. The intuitive function may partly spot a springboard for inspiration in the text and partly get it wrong. For example, the intuitive function might all too easily misread the Lucan account of John the Baptist and see therein the connection with Elijah. The intuitive function might all too easily mishear the divine voice of the Marcan account of the baptism of Jesus and see therein the failure of the crowd to respond. Yet once the sensing function has established the foundations of the narrative, the intuitive function is needed to draw the connections, to establish the links and to build bridges with disparate and contemporary experience. Without the inspiration of the intuitive function, the text remains locked in the biblical past. It is the intuitive function which enables the contemporary people of God to interpret their developing narrative in light of what their God has said and done in the past as recorded through the words of scripture.

While the sensing and the intuitive functions are concerned with perception, the other two functions are concerned with evaluation (thinking and feeling). The SIFT method deals with the feeling function before the thinking function, because the feeling function helps to lay bare some of the issues which the thinking function needs subsequently to analyse. The discipline of feeling ensures that the given passage is fully and properly analysed from the perspective of the participants. The feeling function raises questions about the human motivation, the human values and the personal and interpersonal consequences explicit or implicit in the narrative. For example, the feeling function would be concerned to walk the banks of the Jordan River in John the Baptist's sandals and to experience the encounter with Jesus as John himself experienced it. The feeling function would be conscious of the blood ties between the two men, as symbolized in Luke's account of the relationship between Mary and Elizabeth, their two mothers. The feeling function would be conscious of the implications for John being the forerunner whose destiny was to be overshadowed by the one whose way he came to prepare. Here are enormous human themes of loyalty, of humility and of determination.

According to the SIFT method, the thinking function is brought into play last of all. The discipline of thinking ensures that the crucial issues of truth, of logic and of theology are all properly addressed. The data and the information exposed by the sensing function, the ideas, the theories and the visions so ably spun by the intuitive function, and the stories of human motivations, of human values and of personal and interpersonal consequences so pertinently displayed by the feeling function, are all likely to raise intriguing questions of crucial interest and importance to the thinking function. The discipline of thinking will be curious about potential discrepancies within the given narrative or discontinuity between the given narrative and other parts of scripture, Christian doctrine or contemporary experience. For preachers shaped within conservative theological traditions and for preachers shaped within liberal theological traditions, the thinking function may well raise somewhat different kinds of questions and lead to somewhat different kinds of answers. Yet for both, the thinking function is operating with the same concerns for truth and with the same concerns for the intellectual coherence of the faith.

Testing the SIFT method

So far the SIFT method of biblical hermeneutics and liturgical preaching has been displayed as a set of abstract principles. A good theory, however, needs to be tested and to be displayed in practice before it can be trusted and recommended. This is why it is important that this book has been written by people who are themselves committed to preaching week by week within stable congregations. There they have the opportunity and the responsibility to be actively engaged with the hermeneutical process and with reading the Bible, reading the Spirit and reading the context. One of the authors (Leslie) began using the method in the early 1990s and benefitted greatly from the feedback of the people among whom he worked.

The real challenge to test the method came in conversation between Leslie and Bishop Peter Atkins (then Principal of St John's College, Auckland, New Zealand). At that time the method was being honed on the interpretation of the Gospel passages at the principal Sunday Eucharist. Together they agreed that, if the method was robust, it should be possible to apply the method to each of the passages set for the principal Sunday Gospel reading throughout the three-year cycle proposed by the Revised Common Lectionary. The results of applying the method to over 150 Gospel passages have been published in their series of three books on the lectionary cycles of Matthew, Mark (including Johannine passages) and Luke (Francis and Atkins, 2000, 2001, 2002). These three volumes have stood the test of time.

The second way in which the SIFT method of biblical hermeneutics and liturgical preaching has been tested has been through a series of articles and book chapters which have held the method properly open to peer critique (see for example, Francis, 2003, 2006a, 2006b, 2007b). Again the feedback has been encouraging.

Applying the SIFT method

Having discussed the theoretical foundations and set out the processes by which the SIFT method of biblical hermeneutics and liturgical preaching has been tested and developed, we are ready to display the theory at work. For this purpose we return to an analysis of Mark 4.35–41 (Stilling of the Storm), the passage on which we focused attention in Part 1.

Sensing

The sensing function is concerned with getting the information sorted out and with getting the facts lined up in a row. So become sensing people and make sure that you have put Mark 4.35–41 into context. As sensing people, hear the text, 'On that day, when evening had come.' Quite a lot has already taken place in the earlier verses of Mark's Gospel and you need to remember all that before this passage makes sense.

Become sensing people and remember how Mark sets the scene as soon as John had been arrested (1.14–15). Jesus came 'proclaiming the Gospel of God' and saying 'the Kingdom of God is upon you'. Already by the end of chapter 4 you have experienced three powerful signs of the presence of the Kingdom of God: the call of disciples, the restoration to wholeness, and the proclamation of the Word.

Become sensing people and see the disciples called. See Simon Peter and his brother Andrew at work with a casting net; and see them leave their boat to follow Jesus. See John and his brother James overhauling their nets; and see them leave their boat to follow Jesus. See Levi at work in the custom-house; and see him leave his office to follow Jesus. See all twelve called and named. Open your eyes, for here is irrefutable evidence of God's reign.

Become sensing people and witness the restoration to wholeness. See the possessed man appear in the synagogue at Capernaum; and see the unclean spirit convulse the man and go. See the leper approach, kneel and beg for help; and see Jesus send him away cleansed. See the paralysed man let down through the roof on a stretcher; and see him pick up his stretcher and walk away whole. Open your eyes, for here is irrefutable evidence of God's reign.

Become sensing people and listen to the teaching. Hear about how the sower sowed seed, and how some brought forth a hundredfold. Hear about how the lamp is never placed under the meal-tub or under the bed, but on the lamp stand. Hear about how the mustard seed is the smallest of seeds at its sowing, but grows into the tallest of shrubs. Prick up your ears, for here is irrefutable evidence of God's reign.

Now with all this background you are ready to hear Jesus' call, 'Let us go across to the other side'; you are ready to get into the boat and to trust God's reign. Once in that boat, become sensing people and savour fully the terror of the tempest.

- Hear the roaring wind whipped up all around you.
- See the rolling waves building up all over the lake.
- Feel the frail timbers of the boat rock and shake.
- Smell the danger in the air.
- Taste the terror in the boat.

Become sensing people and recognize that this is no ordinary everyday storm. Listen to the command 'Peace! Be still!' and recognize that this is no ordinary everyday interaction with the forces of nature. Experience the great calm and newly created order, and recognize that this is no ordinary everyday occurrence. Open your eyes, prick up your ears, for here is irrefutable evidence of God's reign.

Intuition

The intuitive function is concerned with grasping the possibilities, and with exploring the connections between one idea and another. So become intuitive people and make sure that you can forge the links between Mark 4.35–41 and what the Spirit is saying to you and to the churches today. As intuitive people, hear the text of invitation, 'Let us go across to the other side.' Here is a Gospel that calls us to openness, to adventure and to change. Indeed, that call to openness, to adventure and to change is the dominant theme of all that has happened so far in Mark's Gospel.

Become intuitive people and revisit Jesus' call to Simon Peter. Here is the invitation to leave behind nets and boats; to leave behind a well-established way of life; to leave behind family and friends; to leave behind wife and mother-in-law. Here is a radical new beginning for personal lives, and the way ahead was by no means storm free. So what aspects of your personal life is Jesus calling you to leave behind when he issues the call, 'Let us go across to the other side'? And what storms will you confront on the way?

Become intuitive people and revisit Jesus' call to Levi. Here is the invitation to re-evaluate priorities; to re-evaluate a whole lifestyle; to re-evaluate the value of a religious commitment once forsaken; to re-evaluate the role in life for wealth and personal gain. Here is a radical new beginning for social and religious values, and the way ahead was by no means storm free. So what among your values and priorities is Jesus calling you to re-evaluate when he issues the call, 'Let us go across to the other side'? And what storms will you confront on the way?

Become intuitive people and revisit Jesus' interaction with the religious leaders of his day. Here is the invitation to reassess how the Sabbath is used; to reassess how healing and freedom can be offered; to reassess how sinners can be welcomed and restored; to reassess how forgiveness can be proclaimed and claimed. Here is a radical new beginning for religious faith, religious teaching and religious law, and the way ahead was by no means storm free. So what among your most dearly held and cherished beliefs is Jesus calling you to reassess when he issues the call, 'Let us go across to the other side'? And what storms will you confront on the way?

Feeling

The feeling function is concerned with what it is to be fully human and with the rich relational connections between individuals. So become feeling people and make sure that you can place yourselves in the shoes of the characters in the narrative of Mark 4.35–41. As feeling people, hear the text of heartfelt anguish, 'Teacher, do you not care that we are perishing?' Here is a Gospel that faces life as it really is and that tells the experience as it really wracks the human heart.

Become feeling people and experience how in the terror of the storm the disciples replayed their experience of discipleship. Jesus had disrupted personal lives when James and John left Zebedee behind in the boat, and when Simon left his wife and mother-in-law behind in the house. Was all this personal change to be lost in the storm; and who cares?

Jesus had disrupted professional lives when fishermen hung up their oars, and when a tax collector walked out of his office. Was all this professional change to be lost in the storm; and who cares?

Jesus had disrupted social lives when people from different walks of life were pressed together in the same boat, when the Zealot and the tax collector became companions in the Kingdom of God. Was all this social change to be lost in the storm; and who cares?

Jesus had disrupted belief systems when the teaching of the law was stood on its head, when the outcasts became accepted and when the righteous were pushed to the margins. Was all this religious change to be lost in the storm; and who cares?

Become feeling people and experience how in the terror of the storm the disciples recognized the rocky side of discipleship for what it truly is. They had been challenged by unclean spirits crying out in the synagogue. They had been challenged by the sick longing for healing. They had been challenged by teachers of the law debating forgiveness. They had been challenged by Pharisees because they had eaten with Levi, because they had plucked corn on the Sabbath, because their Lord was revealing the reign of God. Now even the elements, the wind and the water, were stirred up against them.

Do you not recognize points of your own Christian pilgrimage in that self-same boat, and do you not with them cry aloud, 'Teacher, do you not care that we are perishing?'

Thinking

The thinking function is concerned with logic, with testing truth claims and with objectivity. So become thinking people and make sure that you can test the coherence, the logic and the theology of Mark 4.35–41. As thinking people, hear the text of profound theological importance, 'Who is this, that even the wind and the sea obey him?' Here is a Gospel that poses the ultimate and the fundamental question of the Christian faith.

Become thinking people and assess the evidence as it has been placed before you by Mark. The evidence is that he came into Galilee, proclaiming the gospel of God. So who could do that? The evidence is that he called new leaders for the twelve tribes of Israel (or thirteen, depending on what you make of Levi and of the Levites in the Old Testament). So who could do that? The evidence is that he offers a new kind of teaching and does that with authority. So who could do that?

Become thinking people and assess the evidence as it has been placed before you by Mark. The evidence is that he is demonstrating the reign of God by exorcism and by healing. So who could do that? The evidence is that he is redefining the will of God by displaying release from sin and by liberalizing the Sabbath. So who could do that? The evidence is that his authority stretches over the raging of the seas, the roaring of the winds and the primordial forces of chaos. So who could do that?

Become thinking people, anticipate the question soon to be asked of the disciples, 'Who do you say I am?'; and assess the adequacy of Peter's response, 'You are the Messiah.' Today people are asking and being asked that very same question, 'Who do you say I am?'; but do the old answers continue to suffice?

Conclusion

By taking Mark 4.35–41 as an applied example, this chapter has set out to illustrate the SIFT method of biblical hermeneutics and liturgical preaching, focusing attention on what happens when the four distinctive voices of the Jungian functions (sensing, intuition, feeling and thinking) engage with the same passage of scripture. In this example, the reader has been invited to step inside the biblical narrative (sensing), to engage with the Gospel call for transformation (intuition), to experience and to accept the turbulence of discipleship (feeling), and to face the central Christological question of faith (thinking). In this sense, one passage speaks in diverse ways and fulfils its potential to engage with the beliefs, practices and daily lives of the people of God who are going about building and displaying the reign of God in their own highly contextualized situations.

The hermeneutical process required by the SIFT method requires each preferred voice to be set alongside three other distinctive voices to which equal revelatory authority needs to be given. Thus, for example,

the voice of conservatism preferred by the sensing function is systematically alongside the voice of innovation preferred by the intuitive
function, while the voice of mercy preferred by the feeling function is set
systematically alongside the voice of justice preferred by the thinking
function. In this way the dominical command to love the Lord your God
with all your mind may lead to a richer interpretation of scripture relevant to the specific situation and relevant to the specific context in which
the preacher is located.

The hermeneutical process required by the SIFT method has been
grounded in three basic principles which involve taking seriously the
perspective of the reader, the theology of individual differences and the
insights of psychological type. The method has been developed to help
the people of God hear more clearly the divine revelation that emerges
in the hermeneutical dialogue between the Gospel text and the reader,
preacher or listener. If this aim is achieved, then the link between
psychology and faith, between psychologist and theologian, has been
well worthwhile.

Appendix

Francis Psychological Type Scales

The Francis Psychological Type Scales were developed primarily as a research tool to promote the empirical examination of hypotheses generated by Jungian psychological type theory. They are provided here to help readers to explore and to examine their personal type preferences.

It needs to be made clear that this instrument is not the Myers-Briggs Type Indicator and it does not claim to act as a proxy for the Myers-Briggs Type Indicator. Readers who are specifically interested in learning their Myers-Briggs Type Indicator type are urged to contact a qualified Myers-Briggs Type Indicator practitioner and to complete one of the current tests sold by Myers-Briggs Type Indicator licensed publishers.

The copyright of the Francis Psychological Type Scales (FPTS) is vested in Leslie J. Francis. Users of this book may make copies of the questionnaire for their own personal use in order to explore the application of psychological type for hermeneutics. For all other purposes, written permission must be obtained from the copyright holder by writing to: Professor Leslie J. Francis, Professor of Religions and Education, Warwick Religions and Education Research Unit, Institute of Education, The University of Warwick, Coventry CV4 7AL.

The following list contains pairs of characteristics. For each pair tick (✔) *one* box next to that characteristic which is *closer* to the real you, even if you feel both characteristics apply to you. Tick the characteristic that reflects the real you, even if other people see you differently.

PLEASE COMPLETE EVERY QUESTION

Do you tend to be more . . .

active ☐ *or* ☐ reflective

Do you tend to be more . . .

interested in facts ☐ *or* ☐ interested in theories

Do you tend to be more . . .

concerned for harmony ☐ *or* ☐ concerned for justice

Do you tend to be more . . .

happy with routine ☐ *or* ☐ unhappy with routine

Are you more . . .

private ☐ *or* ☐ sociable

Are you more . . .

inspirational ☐ *or* ☐ practical

Are you more . . .

analytic ☐ *or* ☐ sympathetic

Are you more . . .

structured ☐ *or* ☐ open-ended

Do you prefer . . .

having many friends ☐ *or* ☐ a few deep friendships

Do you prefer . . .

the concrete ☐ *or* ☐ the abstract

Do you prefer . . .

feeling ☐ *or* ☐ thinking

Do you prefer . . .

to act on impulse ☐ *or* ☐ to act on decisions

Do you . . .

dislike parties ☐ *or* ☐ like parties

Do you . . .

       prefer to design ☐ *or* ☐ prefer to make

Do you . . .

       tend to be firm ☐ *or* ☐ tend to be gentle

Do you . . .

       like to be in control ☐ *or* ☐ like to be adaptable

Are you . . .

       energized by others ☐ *or* ☐ drained by too many people

Are you . . .

       conventional ☐ *or* ☐ inventive

Are you . . .

       critical ☐ *or* ☐ affirming

Are you . . .

       happier working alone ☐ *or* ☐ happier working in groups

Do you tend to be more . . .

       socially detached ☐ *or* ☐ socially involved

Do you tend to be more . . .

       concerned for meaning ☐ *or* ☐ concerned about detail

Do you tend to be more . . .

       logical ☐ *or* ☐ humane

Do you tend to be more . . .

       orderly ☐ *or* ☐ easygoing

Are you more . . .

       talkative ☐ *or* ☐ reserved

Are you more . . .

       sensible ☐ *or* ☐ imaginative

Are you more . . .

tactful ☐ *or* ☐ truthful

Are you more . . .

spontaneous ☐ *or* ☐ organized

Are you mostly . . .

an introvert ☐ *or* ☐ an extravert

Are you mostly focused on . . .

present realities ☐ *or* ☐ future possibilities

Are you mostly . . .

trusting ☐ *or* ☐ sceptical

Are you mostly . . .

leisurely ☐ *or* ☐ punctual

Do you . . .

speak before thinking ☐ *or* ☐ think before speaking

Do you prefer to . . .

improve things ☐ *or* ☐ keep things as they are

Do you . . .

seek for truth ☐ *or* ☐ seek for peace

Do you . . .

dislike detailed planning ☐ *or* ☐ like detailed planning

Are you . . .

happier with uncertainty ☐ *or* ☐ happier with certainty

Are you . . .

up in the air ☐ *or* ☐ down to earth

Are you . . .

warm-hearted ☐ *or* ☐ fair-minded

Are you . . .

systematic ☐ *or* ☐ casual

Scoring the Francis Psychological Type Scales

The Francis Psychological Type Scales were designed to present ten pairs of items to differentiate each of the four choices between extraversion and introversion, between sensing and intuition, between thinking and feeling, and between judging and perceiving. The four sets of ten items were then jumbled up so that the purpose behind each pair of items was not too transparent.

Our task now is to unscramble the pairs of items so that we can see more clearly how the test works and so that you can complete your scores. Each set of items will now be taken in turn.

Introversion and extraversion

Find the pairs of items in the Francis Psychological Type Scales which are listed in Table 1. Where you have placed a tick in the box against the response, enter the value 1 in Table 1. Where you have left the box blank, enter the value 0. These are the items designed to differentiate between preferences for extraversion and for introversion. Now add up the two columns. The higher of the two scores indicates your psychological preference, and the difference between the two scores indicates the clarity of your preference between extraversion and introversion. If both columns add up to five, then count yourself as preferring introversion.

Table 1: Orientation

Extraversion				Introversion
active	☐	or	☐	reflective
sociable	☐	or	☐	private
having many friends	☐	or	☐	a few deep friendships
likes parties	☐	or	☐	dislikes parties
energized by others	☐	or	☐	drained by too many people
happier working in groups	☐	or	☐	happier working alone
socially involved	☐	or	☐	socially detached
talkative	☐	or	☐	reserved
an extravert	☐	or	☐	an introvert
speak before thinking	☐	or	☐	think before speaking
Total E score				*Total I score*

Sensing and intuition

Find the pairs of items in the Francis Psychological Type Scales which are listed in Table 2. Where you have placed a tick in the box against the response, enter the value 1 in Table 2. Where you have left the box blank, enter the value 0. These are the items designed to differentiate between preferences for sensing and for intuition. Now add up the two columns. The higher of the two scores indicates your psychological preference, and the difference between the two scores indicates the clarity of your preference between sensing and intuition. If both columns add up to five, then count yourself as preferring intuition.

Table 2: Perceiving process

Sensing				*Intuition*
interested in facts	☐	*or*	☐	interested in theories
practical	☐	*or*	☐	inspirational
the concrete	☐	*or*	☐	the abstract
prefer to make	☐	*or*	☐	prefer to design
conventional	☐	*or*	☐	inventive
concerned about detail	☐	*or*	☐	concerned for meaning
sensible	☐	*or*	☐	imaginative
present realities	☐	*or*	☐	future possibilities
keep things as they are	☐	*or*	☐	improve things
down to earth	☐	*or*	☐	up in the air
Total S score				*Total N score*

Thinking and feeling

Find the pairs of items in the Francis Psychological Type Scales which are listed in Table 3. Where you have placed a tick in the box against the response, enter the value 1 in Table 3. Where you have left the box blank, enter the value 0. These are the items designed to differentiate between preferences for thinking and for feeling. Now add up the two columns. The higher of the two scores indicates your psychological preference, and the difference between the two scores indicates the clarity of your preference between feeling and thinking. If both columns add up to five, then count yourself as preferring feeling.

Table 3: Judging process

Thinking				*Feeling*
concern for justice	☐	*or*	☐	concern for harmony
analytic	☐	*or*	☐	sympathetic
thinking	☐	*or*	☐	feeling
tend to be firm	☐	*or*	☐	tend to be gentle
critical	☐	*or*	☐	affirming
logical	☐	*or*	☐	humane
truthful	☐	*or*	☐	tactful
sceptical	☐	*or*	☐	trusting
seek for truth	☐	*or*	☐	seek for peace
fair-minded	☐	*or*	☐	warm-hearted
Total T score				*Total F score*

Judging and perceiving

Find the pairs of items in the Francis Psychological Type Scales which are listed in Table 4. Where you have placed a tick in the box against the response, enter the value 1 in Table 4. Where you have left the box blank, enter the value 0. These are the items designed to differentiate between preferences for judging and for perceiving. Now add up the two columns. The higher of the two scores indicates your psychological preference, and the difference between the two scores indicates the clarity of your preference between judging and perceiving. If both columns add up to five, then count yourself as preferring perceiving.

Table 4: Attitude toward the outer world

Judging				*Perceiving*
happy with routine	☐	*or*	☐	unhappy with routine
structured	☐	*or*	☐	open-ended
act on decisions	☐	*or*	☐	act on impulse
like to be in control	☐	*or*	☐	like to be adaptable
orderly	☐	*or*	☐	easygoing
organized	☐	*or*	☐	spontaneous
punctual	☐	*or*	☐	leisurely
like detailed planning	☐	*or*	☐	dislike detailed planning
happier with certainty	☐	*or*	☐	happier with uncertainty
systematic	☐	*or*	☐	casual
Total J score				*Total P score*

Notes

Chapter 1

1 See, for example, Adam (2004), Adam, Fowl, Vahhoozer and Watson (2006), Fowl (1997, 1998), Green (1995, 2000), Green and Turner (2000), Vanhoozer (1998, 2006) and Watson (1994, 1997).

Chapter 2

1 Solipsism is the theory that objective reality is unattainable and that the self is all that can be known to exist.

Chapter 3

1 For overviews of this topic, see Eysenck and Keane (2000, chapter 17). There is a useful historical review in Goldstein and Hogarth (1997).

2 The pioneering work in this field was done by the Nobel laureates Daniel Kahneman and Amos Tversky in the 1970s. It is summarized in Kahneman's Nobel Prize lecture (Kahneman, 2003).

Chapter 5

1 This particular way of understanding the letter to the Galatians follows Betz (1979), Barclay (1988) and others.

References

Adam, A. K. M. (1995) *What is Postmodern Biblical Criticism?* Minneapolis, MN: Fortress Press.

—— (2004) Integral and differential hermeneutics. In C. H. Cosgrove (ed.), *The Meanings We Choose: Hermeneutical Ethics, Indeterminacy and the Conflict of Interpretations* (pp. 24–38). London: T & T Clark.

—— (2006) Poaching on Zion: Biblical theology as signifying practice. In A. K. M. Adam, S. E. Fowl, K. J. Vanhoozer and F. Watson (eds), *Reading Scripture with the Church: Toward a Hermeneutic for Theological Interpretation* (pp. 17–34). Grand Rapids, MI: Baker Academic.

Adam, A. K. M., Fowl, S. E., Vanhoozer, K. J. and Watson, F. (eds) (2006) *Reading Scripture with the Church: Toward a Hermeneutic for Theological Interpretation.* Grand Rapids, MI: Baker Academic.

Aichele, G., Burnett, F. W., Castelli, E. A., Fowler, R. M., Jobling, D., Moore, S. D., Phillips, G. A., Pippin, T., Schwartz, R. M. and Wuellner, W. (eds) (1995) *The Postmodern Bible.* New Haven, CT: Yale University Press.

Allen, R. J. (2004) Preaching as mutual critical correlation through conversation. In J. Childers (ed.) *The Purposes of Preaching* (pp. 1–22). St Louis, MO: Chalice Press.

Anderson, J. C. and Moore, S. D. (eds) (1992) *Mark and Method: New Approaches in Biblical Studies.* Minneapolis, MN: Fortress Press.

Barclay, J. M. G. (1988) *Obeying the Truth: A Study of Paul's Ethics in Galatians.* Edinburgh: T & T Clark.

Barton, J. (ed.) (1998) *The Cambridge Companion to Biblical Interpretation.* Cambridge: Cambridge University Press.

Batson, C. D. and Ventis, W. L. (1982) *The Religious Experience: A Social Psychological Perspective.* New York: Oxford University Press.

Batto, B. F. (1987) The sleeping god: An ancient near eastern motif of divine sovereignty. *Biblica, 68*, 153–177.

Beach, L. R. (ed.) (1998) *Image Theory: Theoretical and Empirical Foundations.* Mahwah, NJ: Lawrence Erlbaum Associates.

Betz, H. D. (1979) *Galatians: A Commentary on Paul's Letter to the Churches in Galatia.* Philadelphia, PA: Fortress Press.

Bray, G. (1996) *Biblical Interpretation Past and Present.* Leicester: Apollos/IVP.

Broadbent, D. E. (1958) *Perception and Communication.* New York: Pergamon Press.

Brown, C. G. (2001) *The Death of Christian Britain.* London: Routledge.

Budd, R. J. (1997) *Manual for Jung Type Indicator.* Bedford: Psytech International.

Bultmann, R. (1985) *New Testament & Mythology and Other Basic Writings*. London: SCM Press.

Caprara, G. V. and Cervone, D. (2000) *Personality: Determinands, Dynamics, and Potentials*. Cambridge: Cambridge University Press.

Carrick, J. (2002) *The Imperative of Preaching: A Theology of Sacred Rhetoric*. Edinburgh: Banner of Truth Trust.

Cattell, R. B., Cattell, A. K. S. and Cattell, H. E. P. (1993) *Sixteen Personality Factor Questionnaire: Fifth edition (16PF5)*. Windsor: NFER-Nelson.

Cattell, R. B., Eber, H. W. and Tatsuoka, M. M. (1970) *Handbook for the Sixteen Personality Factor Questionnaire (16PF)*. Champaign, IL: Institute for Personality and Ability Testing.

Coggins, R. J. and Houlden, J. L. (eds) (1990) *A Dictionary of Biblical Interpretation*. London: SCM Press.

Costa, P. T. and McCrae, R. R. (1985) *The NEO Personality Inventory*. Odessa, FL: Psychological Assessment Resources.

Craig, C. L. (2005) Psychological type preferences of rural churchgoers. *Rural Theology*, 3, 123–131.

Craig, C. L., Bigio, J., Robbins, M. and Francis, L. J. (2005) Psychological types of student members of a Christian Union in Wales. *Psychologist in Wales*, 8, 123–131.

Craig, C. L., Duncan, B. and Francis, L. J. (2006a) Psychological type preferences of Roman Catholic priests in the United Kingdom. *Journal of Beliefs and Values*, 27, 157–164.

—— (2006b) Safeguarding tradition: Psychological type preference of male vergers in the Church of England. *Pastoral Psychology*, 54, 457–463.

Craig, C. L., Francis, L. J., Bailey, J. and Robbins, M. (2003) Psychological types in Church in Wales congregations. *The Psychologist in Wales*, 15, 18–21.

Craig, C. L., Francis, L. J. and Barwick, J. (in press) Psychological type preferences of Christian groups: Comparisons with the UK population norms. *Journal of Psychological Type*.

Craig, C. L., Francis, L. J. and Robbins, M. (2004) Psychological type and sex differences among church leaders in the United Kingdom. *Journal of Beliefs and Values*, 25, 3–13.

Craig, C. L., Horsfall, T. and Francis, L. J. (2005) Psychological types of male missionary personnel training in England: A role for thinking type men? *Pastoral Psychology*, 53, 475–482.

Craig, C. L., Williams, A., Francis, L. J. and Robbins, M. (2006) Psychological type and lay ministry among women in the Church in Wales. *Psychologist in Wales*, 19, 3–7.

Cranfield, C. E. B. (1959) *The Gospel According to Saint Mark: An Introduction and Commentary*. Cambridge: Cambridge University Press.

Cranton, P. and Knoop, R. (1995) Assessing Jung's psychological types: The PET Type Check. *Genetic, Social and General Psychology Monographs*, 121, 249–274.

Davies, P. R. (1995) *Whose Bible is it Anyway?* Sheffield: Sheffield Academic Press.

Day, D., Astley, J. and Francis, L. J. (eds) (2005) *A Reader on Preaching: Making Connections*. Aldershot: Ashgate.

Delitzsch, F. J. (1867) *A System of Biblical Psychology* (second edition). Edinburgh: T and T Clark.

Dittes, J. E. (1971) Psychological characteristics of religious professionals. In M. Strommen (ed.) *Research on Religious Development: A Comprehensive Handbook* (pp. 422–460). New York: Hawthorn Books Inc.

Easthope, A. (1991) *Literary into Cultural Studies*. London: Routledge.

Eysenck, H. J. and Eysenck, M. W. (1985) *Personality and Individual Differences: A Natural Science Approach*. New York: Plenum Press.

Eysenck, H. J. and Eysenck, S. B. G. (1991) *Manual of the Eysenck Personality Scales.* London: Hodder and Stoughton.

Eysenck, M. W. and Keane, M. T. (2000) *Cognitive Psychology: A Student's Handbook* (fourth edition). Hove: Psychology Press Ltd.

Fearn, M., Francis, L. J. and Wilcox, C. (2001) Attitude toward Christianity and psychological type: A survey among religious studies students. *Pastoral Psychology, 49,* 341–348.

Fish, S. (1980) *Is There a Text in this Class?* Cambridge, MA: Harvard University Press.

Flemming, D. (2002) Contextualizing the gospel in Athens: Paul's Areopagus address as a paradigm for missionary communication. *Missiology, 30,* 199–214.

Fletcher, M. S. (1912) *The Psychology of the New Testament* (second edition). London: Hodder and Stoughton.

Fowl, S. E. (ed.) (1997) *The Theological Interpretation of Scripture: Classic and Contemporary Readings.* Oxford: Blackwell.

—— (1998) *Engaging Scripture.* Oxford: Blackwell.

Francis, L. J. (1991) The personality characteristics of Anglican ordinands: Feminine men and masculine women? *Personality and Individual Differences, 12,* 1133–1140.

—— (2002) Psychological type and mystical orientation: Anticipating individual differences within congregational life. *Sciences Pastorales, 21*(1), 77–93.

—— (2003) Psychological type and biblical hermeneutics: SIFT method of preaching. *Rural Theology, 1*(1), 13–23.

—— (2005) *Faith and Psychology: Personality, Religion and the Individual.* London: Darton, Longman and Todd.

—— (2006a) Psychological type and liturgical preaching: The SIFT method. *Liturgy, 21*(3), 11–20.

—— (2006b) Mark and psychological type. In J. Vincent (ed.), *Mark's Gospel of Action: Personal and Community Responses* (pp. 98–108). London: SPCK.

—— (2007a) Introducing the New Indices of Religious Orientation (NIRO): Conceptualisation and measurement. *Mental Health, Religion and Culture, 10,* 585–602.

—— (2007b) Psychological types. In F. Watts (ed.), *Jesus and Psychology* (pp. 137–154). London: Darton, Longman and Todd.

Francis, L. J. and Atkins, P. (2000) *Exploring Luke's Gospel: A Guide to the Gospel Readings in the Revised Common Lectionary.* London: Mowbray.

—— (2001) *Exploring Matthew's Gospel: A Guide to the Gospel Readings in the Revised Common Lectionary.* London: Mowbray.

—— (2002) *Exploring Mark's Gospel: An Aid for Readers and Preachers Using Year B of the Revised Common Lectionary.* London: Continuum.

Francis, L. J., Butler, A. and Craig, C. L. (2005) Understanding the Parochial Church Council: Dynamics of psychological type and gender. *Contact, 147,* 25–32.

Francis, L. J., Butler, A., Jones, S. H. and Craig, C. L. (2007) Type patterns among active members of the Anglican church: A perspective from England. *Mental Health, Religion and Culture, 10,* 435–443.

Francis, L. J., Craig, C. L. and Butler, A. (2007) Psychological types of male evangelical Anglican seminarians in England. *Journal of Psychological Type, 67,* 11–17.

Francis, L. J., Craig, C. L., Horsfall, T. and Ross, C. F. J. (2005) Psychological types of male and female evangelical lay church leaders in England, compared with United Kingdom population norms. *Fieldwork in Religion, 1,* 69–83.

Francis, L. J., Craig, C. L., Whinney, M., Tilley, D. and Slater, P. (2007) Psychological profiling of Anglican clergy in England: Employing Jungian typology to interpret diversity, strengths, and potential weaknesses in ministry. *International Journal of Practical Theology.*

Francis, L. J., Duncan, B., Craig, C. L. and Luffman, G. (2004) Type patterns among Anglican congregations in England. *Journal of Adult Theological Education, 1*(1), 65–77.

Francis, L. J. and Jones, S. H. (1997) Personality and charismatic experience among adult Christians. *Pastoral Psychology, 45*, 421–428.

—— (1998) Personality and Christian belief among adult churchgoers. *Journal of Psychological Type, 47*, 5–11.

—— (1999) Psychological type and tolerance for religious uncertainty. *Pastoral Psychology, 47*, 253–259.

Francis, L. J., Jones, S. H. and Craig, C. L. (2004) Personality and religion: The relationship between psychological type and attitude toward Christianity. *Archiv Für Religionspsychologie, 26*, 15–33.

Francis, L. J. and Kay, W. K. (1995) The personality characteristics of Pentecostal ministry candidates. *Personality and Individual Differences, 18*, 581–594.

—— (in press) Psychological type preferences of female Bible College students in England.

Francis, L. J., Lewis, J. M., Brown, L. B., Philipchalk, R. and Lester, D. (1995) Personality and religion among undergraduate students in the United Kingdom, United States, Australia and Canada. *Journal of Psychology and Christianity, 14*, 250–262.

Francis, L. J., Lewis, J. M., Philipchalk, R., Brown, L. B. and Lester, D. (1995) The internal consistency reliability and construct validity of the Francis Scale of Attitude toward Christianity (adult) among undergraduate students in the UK, USA, Australia and Canada. *Personality and Individual Differences, 19*, 949–953.

Francis, L. J. and Louden, S. H. (2000a) The Francis-Louden Mystical Orientation Scale (MOS): A study among Roman Catholic priests. *Research in the Social Scientific Study of Religion, 11*, 99–116.

—— (2000b) Mystical orientation and psychological type: A study among student and adult churchgoers. *Transpersonal Psychology Review, 4*(1), 36–42.

Francis, L. J., Nash, P., Nash, S. and Craig, C. L. (2007) Psychology and youth ministry: Psychological type preferences of Christian youth workers in the United Kingdom. *Journal of Youth Ministry, 5*(2), 73–90.

Francis, L. J., Payne, V. J. and Jones, S. H. (2001) Psychological types of male Anglican clergy in Wales. *Journal of Psychological Type, 56*, 19–23.

Francis, L. J. and Pegg, S. (2007), Psychological type profile of female volunteer workers in a rural Christian charity shop, *Rural Theology, 5*, 53–56.

Francis, L. J., Penson, A. W. and Jones, S. H. (2001) Psychological types of male and female Bible college students in England. *Mental Health, Religion and Culture, 4*, 23–32.

Francis, L. J. and Robbins, M. (2002) Psychological types of male evangelical church leaders. *Journal of Beliefs and Values, 23*, 217–220.

—— (2003) Personality and glossolalia: A study among male Evangelical clergy. *Pastoral Psychology, 51*, 391–396.

—— (2004) *Personality and Pastoral Care: A Study in Empirical Theology*. Cambridge: Grove Books.

Francis, L. J., Robbins, M., Boxer, A., Lewis, C. A., McGuckin, C. and McDaid, C. J. (2003) Psychological type and attitude toward Christianity: A replication. *Psychological Reports, 92*, 89–90.

Francis, L. J., Robbins, M., Williams, A. and Williams, R. (2007) All types are called, but some are more likely to respond: The psychological profile of rural Anglican churchgoers in Wales. *Rural Theology, 5*, 23–30.

Francis, L. J. and Ross, C. F. J. (1997) The perceiving function and Christian spirituality: Distinguishing between sensing and intuition. *Pastoral Sciences, 16*, 93–103.

—— (2000) Personality type and quest orientation of religiosity. *Journal of Psychological Type, 55*, 22–25.

Francis, L. J. and Thomas, T. H. (1997) Are charismatic ministers less stable? A study among male Anglican clergy. *Review of Religious Research, 39*, 61–69.

Francis, L. J., Village, A., Robbins, M. and Ineson, K. (2007) Mystical orientation and psychological type: An empirical study among guests staying at a Benedictine Abbey. *Studies in Spirituality.*

Funder, D. C. (1997) *The Personality Puzzle.* New York: WW Norton.

Gadamer, H.-G. (1960) *Truth and Method* (English translation 1975). London: Sheed & Ward.

Galotti, K. M. (2007) Decision structuring in important real-life choices. *Psychological Science, 18*, 320–325.

Geyer, D. W. (2002) *Fear, Anomaly, and Uncertainty in the Gospel of Mark.* Lanham, MD: Scarecrow Press.

Gillingham, S. E. (1998) *One Bible Many Voices.* London: SPCK.

Goldstein, W. M. and Hogarth, R. M. (eds) (1997) *Research on Judgment and Decision Making: Currents, Connections, and Controversies.* Cambridge: Cambridge University Press.

Gray, H. and Wheelwright, J. B. (1946) Jung's psychological types, their frequency of occurrence. *Journal of General Psychology, 34*, 3–17.

Green, J. B. (1995) *Hearing the New Testament: Strategies for Interpretation.* Grand Rapids, MI: Eerdmans.

—— (2000) Scripture and theology: Uniting the two so long divided. In J. B. Green and M. Turner (eds), *Between Two Horizons: Spanning New Testament Studies and Systematic Theology* (pp. 23–43). Grand Rapids, MI: Eerdmans.

Green, J. B. and Turner, M. (eds) (2000) *Between Two Horizons: Spanning New Testament Studies and Systematic Theology.* Grand Rapids, MI: Eerdmans.

Guerin, W. L., Labor, E., Morgan, L., Reesman, J. C. and Willingham, J. R. (2005) *A Handbook of Critical Approaches to Literature* (fifth edition). New York: Oxford University Press.

Hall, G. S. (1917) *Jesus, the Christ in the Light of Psychology* (two volumes). Garden City, NY: Doubleday.

Hayes, J. H. (ed.) (1999) *Dictionary of Biblical Interpretation.* Nashville, TN: Abingdon Press.

Haynes, S. R. and McKenzie, S. C. (eds) (1999) *To Each His Own Meaning: An Introduction to Biblical Criticisms and Their Applications* (second edition). Louisville, KY: Westminster John Knox Press.

Heisler, G. (2007) *Spirit-led Preaching: The Holy Spirit's Role in Sermon Preparation and Delivery.* Nashville, TN: B&H Publishing Group.

Hirsch, E. D. J. (1967) *Validity in Interpretation.* New Haven, CT: Yale University Press.

—— (1976) *The Aims of Interpretation.* Chicago: University of Chicago Press.

Hogan, R., Johnson, J. and Briggs, S. (eds) (1997) *Handbook of Personality Psychology.* New York: Academic Press.

James, W. (1902) *The Varieties of Religious Experience.* New York: Longmans Green.

Johnson, L. T. (1996) *Scripture and Discernment.* Nashville, TN: Abingdon Press.

Jones, S. H. and Francis, L. J. (1999) Personality type and attitude toward Christianity among student churchgoers. *Journal of Beliefs and Values, 20*, 105–109.

Jones, S. H., Francis, L. J. and Craig, C. L. (2005) Charismatic experience and psychological type: An empirical enquiry. *Journal of the European Pentecostal Theological Association, 25,* 39–53.

Jung, C. G. (1971) *Psychological Types: The Collected Works, Volume 6.* London: Routledge and Kegan Paul.

Kahneman, D. (2003) A perspective on judgment and choice: Mapping bounded rationality. *American Psychologist, 58,* 697–720.

Kay, W. K. (2000) *Pentecostals in Britain.* Carlisle: Paternoster.

Kay, W. K., Francis, L. J. and Craig, C. L. (in press) Psychological type preferences of male British Assemblies of God Bible College students: Tough-minded or tender-hearted? *Journal of the European Pentecostal Theological Association.*

Keirsey, D. (1998) *Please Understand Me: 2.* Del Mar, CA: Prometheus Nemesis.

Keirsey, D. and Bates, M. (1978) *Please Understand Me.* Del Mar, CA: Prometheus Nemesis.

Kendall, E. (1998) *Myers-Briggs Type Indicator: Step 1 Manual Supplement.* Palo Alto, CA: Consulting Psychologists Press.

Kier, F. J., Melancon, J. G. and Thompson, B. (1998) Reliability and validity of scores on the Personal Preferences Self-Description Questionnaire (PPSDQ). *Educational and Psychological Measurement, 58,* 612–622.

King, U. (ed.) (1996) *Feminist Theology from the Third World: A Reader.* London: SPCK.

Kitzberger, I. R. (ed.) (1999) *The Personal Voice in Biblical Interpretation.* London: Routledge.

Kysar, R. and Webb, J. M. (2006) *Preaching to Postmoderns: New Perspectives for Proclaiming the Message.* Edinburgh: Alban Books Limited.

Long, T. G. (1989) *The Witness of Preaching.* Louisville, KY: Westminster John Knox Press.

Loomis, M. (1982) A new perspective for Jung's typology: The Singer-Loomis Inventory of Personality. *Journal of Analytical Psychology, 27,* 59–69.

Losie, L. A. (2004) Paul's speech on the Areopagus: A model of cross-cultural evangelism: Acts 17:16–34. In R. L. Gallagher and P. Hertig (eds), *Mission in Acts: Ancient Narratives in Contemporary Context* (pp. 221–238). Maryknoll, NY: Orbis Books.

Louden, S. H. and Francis, L. J. (1999) The personality profile of Roman Catholic parochial secular priests in England and Wales. *Review of Religious Research, 41,* 65–79.

—— (2001) Are Catholic priests in England and Wales attracted to the charismatic movement emotionally less stable? *British Journal of Theological Education, 11,* 65–76.

Malbon, E. S. (1992) Narrative criticism: How does the story mean? In J. C. Anderson and S. D. Moore (eds), *Mark and Method* (pp. 23–49). Minneapolis, MN: Fortress Press.

Matera, F. (1988) The prologue to Mark's gospel. *Journal for the Study of the New Testament, 34,* 3–20.

McCartney, D. and Clayton, C. (1994) *Let the Reader Understand: A Guide to Interpreting and Applying the Bible.* Grand Rapids, MI: Baker Books.

Mitchell, W. D. (1991) A test of type theory using the TDI. *Journal of Psychological Type, 22,* 15–26.

Morgan, R. with Barton, J. (1988) *Biblical Interpretation.* Oxford: Oxford University Press.

Musson, D. J. (2001) Male and female Anglican clergy: Gender reversal on the 16PF5? *Review of Religious Research, 43,* 175–183.

—— (2002) Personality of male Anglican clergy in England: Revisited using the 16PF5. *Mental Health, Religion and Culture, 5,* 195–206.

Myers, I. B. (1998) *Introduction to Type: A Guide to Understanding Your Results on the Myers-Briggs Type Indicator* (fifth edition, European English version). Oxford: Oxford Psychologists Press.

Myers, I. B. and McCaulley, M. H. (1985) *Manual: A Guide to the Development and Use of the Myers-Briggs Type Indicator*. Palo Alto, California: Consulting Psychologists Press.

Myers, I. B., McCaulley, M. H., Quenk, N. L. and Hammer, A. L. (1998) *Manual: A Guide to the Development and Use of the Myers-Briggs Type Indicator*. Palo Alto, CA: Consulting Psychologists Press.

Noble, P. R. (1994) Hermeneutics and post-modernism: Can we have a radical reader-response theory? Part I. *Religious Studies, 30,* 419–436.

—— (1995) Hermeneutics and post-modernism: Can we have a radical reader-response theory? Part II. *Religious Studies, 31,* 1–22.

—— (1996) Fish and the Bible: Should reader-response theories 'catch on'? *Heythrop Journal, 37,* 456–467.

Pagitt, D. (2005) *Beyond Preaching: The Role of the Sermon in Communities of Faith*. New York: HarperCollins Publishers.

Piedmont, R. L. (1999) Strategies for using the five-factor model of personality in religious research. *Journal of Psychology and Theology, 27,* 338–350.

Ramsey, G. L. (2005) *Care-full Preaching: From Sermon to Caring Community*. Saint Louis, MO: Chalice Press.

Rawling, K. (1992) *Preliminary Manual: The Cambridge Type Indicator: Research edition*. Cambridge: Rawling Associates.

Robbins, M., Francis, L. J., Haley, J. M. and Kay, W. K. (2001) The personality characteristics of Methodist ministers: Feminine men and masculine women? *Journal for the Scientific Study of Religion, 40,* 123–128.

Robbins, M., Francis, L. J. and Rutledge, C. (1997) The personality characteristics of Anglican stipendiary parochial clergy in England: Gender differences revisited. *Personality and Individual Differences, 23,* 199–204.

Robbins, M., Hair, J. and Francis, L. J. (1999) Personality and attraction to the charismatic movement: A study among Anglican clergy. *Journal of Beliefs and Values, 20,* 239–246.

Robins, R. W., Fraley, R. C. and Krueger, R. F. (eds) (2007) *Handbook of Research Methods in Personality Psychology*. New York: Guilford Press.

Rollins, W. G. and Kille, D. A. (eds) (2007) *Psychological Insight into the Bible: Texts and Readings*. Grand Rapids, MI: William B Eerdmans.

Ross, C. F. J. and Francis, L. J. (in press) The relationship of intrinsic, extrinsic and quest religious orientation to Jungian psychological type among churchgoers.

Saroglou, V. (2002) Religion and the five factors of personality: a meta-analytic review. *Personality and Individual Differences, 32,* 15–25.

Segovia, F. F. (1995) Cultural studies and contemporary biblical criticism: Ideological criticism as a mode of discourse. In F. F. Segovia and M. A. Tolbert (eds), *Reading from this Place: Social Location and Biblical Interpretation in Global Perspective* (Vol. 2, pp. 1–17). Minneapolis, MN: Fortress Press.

Segovia, F. F. and Tolbert, M. A. (eds) (1995a) *Reading from this Place: Social Location and Biblical Interpretation in Global Perspective* (Vol. 1). Minneapolis, MN: Fortress Press.

—— (eds) (1995b) *Reading from this Place: Social Location and Biblical Interpretation in Global Perspective* (Vol. 2). Minneapolis, MN: Fortress Press.

Shillington, V. G. (2002) *Reading the Sacred Text: An Introduction to Biblical Studies*. London: T & T Clark.

Slee, N. (2003) *Faith and Feminism: An Introduction to Christian Feminist Theology*. London: Darton, Longman and Todd.

—— (2004) *Women's Faith Development: Patterns and Processes*. Aldershot: Ashgate.

Smith, C. (2004) Preaching hospitality, de-centering, re-membering, and right relations. In J. Childers (ed.), *The Purposes of Preaching* (pp. 91–112). St Louis, MO: Chalice Press.

Spilka, B., Hood, R. W. jr., Hunsberger, B. and Gorsuch, R. (2003) *The Psychology of Religion: An Empirical Approach* (third edition). New York: Guilford Press.

Stendahl, K. (1962) Biblical theology, contemporary. In G. A. Buttrick (ed.) *Interpreter's Dictionary of the Bible* (vol. 1, pp. 418–431). Nashville: Abingdon.

—— (ed.) (1995) *Voices from the Margin: Interpreting the Bible in the Third World*. Maryknoll, NY: Orbis/SPCK.

Sugirtharajah, R. S. (2001) *The Bible and the Third World: Precolonial, Colonial, and Postcolonial Encounters*. Cambridge: Cambridge University Press.

Tate, W. R. (1997) *Biblical Interpretation*. Peabody, MA: Hendrickson.

Taylor, V. (1966) *The Gospel According to Mark*. London: Macmillan.

Thiselton, A. C. (1980) *The Two Horizons*. Exeter: Paternoster Press.

—— (1992) *New Horizons in Hermeneutics*. London: HarperCollins.

Tompkins, J. P. (ed.) (1980) *Reader-response Criticism. From Formalism to Post-structuralism*. Baltimore, MD: John Hopkins University Press.

Towler, R. and Coxon, A. P. M. (1979) *The Fate of the Anglican Clergy*. London: Macmillan.

Vanhoozer, K. J. (1998) *Is There a Meaning in this Text?* Leicester: Apollos / IVP.

—— (2006) *Dictionary for Theological Interpretation of the Bible*. London: SPCK Publishing.

Village, A. (2006) Biblical interpretative horizons and ordinary readers: An empirical study. *Research in the Social Scientific Study of Religion, 17*, 157–176.

—— (2007) *The Bible and Lay People: An Empirical Approach to Ordinary Hermeneutics*. Aldershot: Ashgate.

Village, A. and Francis, L. J. (2005) The relationship of psychological type preferences to biblical interpretation. *Journal of Empirical Theology, 18*, 74–89.

Village, A., Francis, L. J. and Craig, C. L. (in press) Church tradition and psychological type preferences among Anglicans in England, *Journal of Anglican Studies*.

Ware, R., Yokomoto, C. and Morris, B. B. (1985) A preliminary study to assess validity of the Personal Style Inventory. *Psychological Reports, 56*, 903–910.

Watson, F. (1994) *Text, Church and World*. Edinburgh: T & T Clark.

—— (1997) *Text and Truth. Redefining Biblical Theology*. Edinburgh: T & T Clark.

Wells, A. and Matthews, G. (1994) *Attention and Emotion: A Clinical Perspective*. Hove: Lawrence Erlbaum Associates.

Index of Subjects

Index of Names